*B*ible
PROMISES

⊞ *Whitaker House*

All Scripture quotations are taken from the *King James Version* (KJV) of the Bible.

BIBLE PROMISES

ISBN: 0-88368-283-4
Printed in the United States of America
Copyright © 1995 by Whitaker House

Whitaker House
30 Hunt Valley Circle
New Kensington, PA 15068

3 4 5 6 7 8 9 10 11 12 / 06 05 04 03 02 01 00 99 98 97

Contents

Bible Promises for Those Who Are...113

Bible Promises for Those Who... 159

Introduction

According as his divine power hath given unto
us all things that pertain unto life and
godliness, through the knowledge of him that
hath called us to glory and virtue: Whereby are
*given unto us **exceeding great and precious***
***promises**: that by these ye might be partakers*
of the divine nature, having escaped the
corruption that is in the world through lust.
—2 Peter 1:3-4

God has given His children a rich inheritance of spiritual, physical, and personal blessings. Further, He has provided us with written documentation of His bequest through the Old and New Testaments, or Covenants, of the Holy Bible.

9

By biblical standards, a covenant is an unbreakable contract which binds the instigator to meet the terms of the agreement, no matter whether the recipient performs according to the contract conditions or not. The greatest covenantal gift God has bestowed on us is salvation and eternal life through the shed blood of His Son, Jesus Christ. Nothing we can do will earn us a position in the kingdom of God. The only way we can respond is simply receive the blessing by faith.

Our Heavenly Father has also made provision for each of us in all facets of our lives. In the following pages, you will find His unbreakable promises to you. As you received salvation by faith, accept these gifts which God offers to you in the same way He provided salvation for anyone who would believe—because He first loved us.

Bible Promises that God Will...

Fulfill His Promises

According as his divine power hath given unto us all things that *pertain* unto life and godliness, through the knowledge of him that hath called us to glory and virtue: Whereby are given unto us exceeding great and precious promises: that by these ye might be partakers of the divine nature. *2 Peter 1:3-4*

For he *is* faithful that promised. *Hebrews 10:23*

Blessed *be* the LORD, that hath given rest unto his people Israel, according to all that he promised: there hath not failed one word of all his good promise. *1 Kings 8:56*

11

The Lord is not slack concerning his promise, as some men count slackness; but is longsuffering to us-ward.   *2 Peter 3:9*

Know therefore that the LORD thy God, he *is* God, the faithful God, which keepeth covenant and mercy with them that love him and keep his commandments to a thousand generations.   *Deuteronomy 7:9*

God *is* not a man, that he should lie; neither the son of man, that he should repent: hath he said, and shall he not do *it*? or hath he spoken, and shall he not make it good?
Numbers 23:19

Nevertheless my lovingkindness will I not utterly take from him, nor suffer my faithfulness to fail. My covenant will I not break, nor alter the thing that is gone out of my lips.
Psalm 89:33-34

And, behold, I send the promise of my Father upon you: but tarry ye in the city of Jerusalem, until ye be endued with power from on high.   *Luke 24:49*

I have spoken *it*, I will also bring it to pass; I have purposed *it*, I will also do it. *Isaiah 46:11*

Thy word *is* true *from* the beginning: and every one of thy righteous judgments *endureth* for ever.   *Psalm 119:160*

For he remembered his holy promise, *and* Abraham his servant. And he brought forth his people with joy, *and* his chosen with gladness: And gave them the lands of the heathen: and they inherited the labor of the people; That they might observe his statutes, and keep his laws. Praise ye the LORD.   *Psalm 105:42-45*

And, being assembled together with *them,* commanded them that they should not depart from Jerusalem, but wait for the promise of the Father, which, *saith he,* ye have heard of me. For John truly baptized with water; but ye shall be baptized with the Holy Ghost not many days hence.   *Acts 1:4-5*

Therefore being by the right hand of God exalted, and having received of the Father the promise of the Holy Ghost, he hath shed forth this, which ye now see and hear.   *Acts 2:33*

For all the promises of God in him *are* yea, and in him Amen, unto the glory of God by us.
          2 Corinthians 1:20

Hear Our Prayers

For the eyes of the Lord *are* over the righteous, and his ears *are open* unto their prayers.
1 Peter 3:12

The righteous cry, and the LORD heareth, and
delivereth them out of all their troubles.
Psalm 34:17

This is the confidence that we have in him,
that if we ask any thing according to his will,
he heareth us.   *1 John 5:14*

But know that the LORD hath set apart him
that is godly for himself: the LORD will hear
when I call unto him.   *Psalm 4:3*

He will regard the prayer of the destitute, and
not despise their prayer.   *Psalm 102:17*

If thou return to the Almighty, thou shalt be
built up, thou shalt put away iniquity far from
thy tabernacles...For then shalt thou have thy
delight in the Almighty, and shalt lift up thy
face unto God. Thou shalt make thy prayer
unto him, and he shall hear thee.
Job 22:23, 26-27

If my people, which are called by my name, shall humble themselves, and pray, and seek my face, and turn from their wicked ways; then will I hear from heaven, and will forgive their sin, and will heal their land.

2 Chronicles 7:14

Respond to Our Prayers

And it shall come to pass, that before they call, I will answer; and while they are yet speaking, I will hear.   *Isaiah 65:24*

Call unto me, and I will answer thee, and show thee great and mighty things, which thou knowest not.   *Jeremiah 33:3*

And if we know that he hear us, whatsoever we ask, we know that we have the petitions that we desired of him.   *1 John 5:15*

Hitherto have ye asked nothing in my name: ask, and ye shall receive, that your joy may be full.   *John 16:24*

If two of you shall agree on earth as touching any thing that they shall ask, it shall be done for them of my Father which is in heaven.

Matthew 18:19

Ask, and it shall be given you; seek, and ye shall find; knock, and it shall be opened unto you: For every one that asketh receiveth; and he that seeketh findeth; and to him that knocketh it shall be opened.   *Matthew 7:7-8*

If ye abide in me, and my words abide in you, ye shall ask what ye will, and it shall be done unto you.   *John 15:7*

Then shalt thou call, and the LORD shall answer; thou shalt cry, and he shall say, Here I am.   *Isaiah 58:9*

Bible Promises for...

Abundance

My God shall supply all your needs according
to his riches in glory by Christ Jesus.
Philippians 4:19

Seek ye first the kingdom of God, and his
righteousness; and all these things shall be
added unto you. *Matthew 6:33*

For the LORD God *is* a sun and shield: the
LORD will give grace and glory: no good *thing*
will he withhold from them that walk uprightly. *Psalm 84:11*

And Hezekiah had exceeding much riches and
honor: and he made himself treasuries for silver, and for gold, and for precious stones, and
for spices, and for shields, and for all manner
of pleasant jewels; Storehouses also for the
increase of corn, and wine, and oil; and stalls
for all manner of beasts, and cotes for flocks.
Moreover he provided him cities, and posses-
sions of flocks and herds in abundance: for
God had given him substance very much.

2 Chronicles 32:27-29

I [wisdom] love them that love me; and those
that seek me early shall find me. Riches and
honor *are* with me; *yea,* durable riches and
righteousness. My fruit *is* better than gold,
yea, than fine gold; and my revenue than
choice silver. I lead in the way of righteousness, in the midst of the paths of judgment:
That I may cause those that love me to inherit
substance; and I will fill their treasures.

Proverbs 8:17-21

For all these things do the nations of the
world seek after: and your Father knoweth
that ye have need of these things. But rather
seek ye the kingdom of God; and all these
things shall be added unto you.

Luke 12:30-31

And it shall come to pass, if thou shalt hearken diligently unto the voice of the LORD thy God, to observe *and* to do all his commandments which I command thee this day...the LORD shall make thee plenteous in goods, in the fruit of thy body, and in the fruit of thy cattle, and in the fruit of thy ground, in the land which the LORD sware unto thy fathers to give thee. The LORD shall open unto thee his good treasure, the heaven to give the rain unto thy land in his season, and to bless all the work of thine hand: and thou shalt lend unto many nations, and thou shalt not borrow. And the LORD shall make thee the head, and not the tail; and thou shalt be above only, and thou shalt not be beneath; if that thou hearken unto the commandments of the LORD thy God, which I command thee this day, to observe and to do *them*.

Deuteronomy 28:1, 11-13

So the children went in and possessed the land...And they took strong cities, and a fat land, and possessed houses full of all goods, wells digged, vineyards, and oliveyards, and fruit trees in abundance: so they did eat, and were filled, and became fat, and delighted themselves in thy great goodness.

Nehemiah 9:24-25

O fear the LORD, ye his saints: for *there is* no want to them that fear him. The young lions do lack, and suffer hunger: but they that seek the LORD shall not want any good *thing*.
Psalm 34:9-10

But the meek shall inherit the earth; and shall delight themselves in the abundance of peace.   *Psalm 37:11*

Children

Lo, children *are* an heritage of the LORD: *and* the fruit of the womb *is his* reward. As arrows *are* in the hand of a mighty man; so *are* children of the youth. Happy *is* the man that hath his quiver full of them.   *Psalm 127:3-5*

In the fear of the LORD *is* strong confidence: and his children shall have a place of refuge.
Proverbs 14:26

The just *man* walketh in his integrity: his children *are* blessed after him.   *Proverbs 20:7*

He maketh the barren woman to keep house, *and to be* a joyful mother of children. Praise ye the LORD.   *Psalm 113:9*

If ye hearken to these judgments, and keep, and do them, that the LORD thy God shall keep unto thee the covenant...he will love thee, and bless thee, and multiply thee: he will also bless the fruit of thy womb...there shall not be male or female barren among you.
Deuteronomy 7:12-14

He will bless them that fear the LORD, *both* small and great. The LORD shall increase you more and more, you and your children.
Psalm 115:13-14

And ye shall serve the LORD your God, and he shall bless thy bread, and thy water...There shall nothing cast their young, nor be barren, in thy land. *Exodus 23:25-26*

Thy wife *shall be* as a fruitful vine by the sides of thine house: thy children like olive plants round about thy table. *Psalm 128:3*

Yet setteth he the poor on high from affliction, and maketh *him* families like a flock.
Psalm 107:41

Children's children *are* the crown of old men; and the glory of children *are* their fathers.
Proverbs 17:6

And I will give them one heart, and one way, that they may fear me for ever, for the good of them, and of their children after them.
Jeremiah 32:39

The father of the righteous shall greatly rejoice: and he that begetteth a wise *child* shall have joy of him. Thy father and thy mother shall be glad, and she that bare thee shall rejoice.
Proverbs 23:24-25

They send forth their little ones like a flock, and their children dance.
Job 21:11

He hath blessed thy children within thee.
Psalm 147:13

For I will pour water upon him that is thirsty, and floods upon the dry ground: I will pour my spirit upon thy seed, and my blessing upon thine offspring.
Isaiah 44:3

And all thy children *shall be* taught of the LORD; and great *shall be* the peace of thy children.
Isaiah 54:13

For the promise is unto you, and to your children, and to all that are afar off, *even* as many as the Lord our God shall call.
Acts 2:39

Comfort

And I will pray the Father, and he shall give you another Comforter, that he may abide with you for ever...I will not leave you comfortless: I will come to you. *John 14:16-18*

I, *even* I, *am* he that comforteth you: who *art* thou, that thou shouldest be afraid of a man *that* shall die, and of the son of man *which* shall be made *as* grass. *Isaiah 51:12*

In the multitude of my thoughts within me thy comforts delight my soul. *Psalm 94:19*

Remember the word unto thy servant, upon which thou hast caused me to hope. This *is* my comfort in my affliction: for thy word hath quickened me. *Psalm 119:49-50*

Sing, O heavens; and be joyful, O earth; and break forth into singing, O mountains: for the LORD hath comforted his people, and will have mercy upon his afflicted. *Isaiah 49:13*

Yea, though I walk through the valley of the shadow of death, I will fear no evil: for thou *art* with me; thy rod and thy staff they comfort me. *Psalm 23:4*

Blessed *be* God, even the Father of our Lord
Jesus Christ, the Father of mercies, and the
God of all comfort; Who comforteth us in all
our tribulation, that we may be able to comfort them which are in any trouble, by the
comfort wherewith we ourselves are com-
forted of God.   *2 Corinthians 1:3-4*

Blessed *are* they that mourn: for they shall be
comforted.   *Matthew 5:4*

The spirit of the Lord GOD *is* upon me; because the LORD hath anointed me...to comfort
all that mourn.   *Isaiah 61:2*

Now our Lord Jesus Christ himself, and God,
even our Father, which hath loved us, and
hath given *us* everlasting consolation and
good hope through grace, Comfort your
hearts, and stablish you in every good word
and work.   *2 Thessalonians 2:16-17*

Thou shalt increase my greatness, and com-
fort me on every side.   *Psalm 71:21*

For whatsoever things were written aforetime
were written for our learning, that we
through patience and comfort of the scrip-
tures might have hope.   *Romans 15:4*

This *is* my comfort in my affliction: for thy word hath quickened me.   *Psalm 119:50*

For the LORD shall comfort Zion: he will comfort all her waste places; and he will make her wilderness like Eden, and her desert like the garden of the LORD; joy and gladness shall be found therein, thanksgiving, and the voice of melody.   *Isaiah 51:3*

Thus saith the LORD of hosts; My cities through prosperity shall yet be spread abroad; and the LORD shall yet comfort Zion, and shall yet choose Jerusalem.   *Zechariah 1:17*

As one whom his mother comforteth, so will I comfort you; and ye shall be comforted in Jerusalem.   *Isaiah 66:13*

For I will turn their mourning into joy, and will comfort them, and make them rejoice from their sorrow.   *Jeremiah 31:13*

If *there be* therefore any consolation in Christ, if any comfort of love, if any fellowship of the Spirit, if any bowels and mercies, Fulfill ye my joy, that ye be like-minded, having the same love, *being* of one accord, of one mind.   *Philippians 2:1-2*

But Jesus turned him about, and when he saw her, he said, Daughter, be of good comfort; thy faith hath made thee whole.   *Matthew 9:22*

Be perfect, be of good comfort, be of one mind, live in peace; and the God of love and peace shall be with you.   *2 Corinthians 13:11*

That their hearts might be comforted, being knit together in love, and unto all riches of the full assurance of understanding, to the acknowledgment of the mystery of God, and of the Father, and of Christ.   *Colossians 2:2*

I have seen his ways, and will heal him: I will lead him also, and restore comforts unto him.
Isaiah 57:18

Confidence

Being confident of this very thing, that he which hath begun a good work in you will perform *it* until the day of Jesus Christ.
Philippians 1:6

For the LORD shall be thy confidence, and shall keep thy foot from being taken.
Proverbs 3:26

By terrible things in righteousness wilt thou answer us, O God of our salvation; *who art* the confidence of all the ends of the earth.

Psalm 65:5

And they shall dwell safely therein, and shall build houses, and plant vineyards; yea, they shall dwell with confidence, when I have executed judgments upon all those that despise them round about them; and they shall know that I *am* the LORD their God.   *Ezekiel 28:26*

For thus saith the Lord GOD, the Holy One of Israel; In returning and rest shall ye be saved; in quietness and in confidence shall be your strength.   *Isaiah 30:15*

This is the confidence that we have in him, that, if we ask any thing according to his will. he heareth us: And if we know that he hears us, whatsoever we ask, we know that we have the petitions that we desired of him.

1 John 5:14-15

Beloved, if our heart condemn us not, *then* have we confidence toward God. And whatsoever we ask, we receive of him, because we keep his commandments, and do those things that are pleasing in his sight.   *1 John 3:21-22*

In whom we have boldness and access with confidence by the faith of him.   *Ephesians 3:12*

In the fear of the LORD *is* strong confidence: and his children shall have a place of refuge.
                                    Proverbs 14:26

Deliverance from Evil

The LORD shall preserve thee from all evil: he shall preserve thy soul.   *Psalm 121:7*

And the Lord shall deliver me from every evil work, and will preserve *me* unto his heavenly kingdom: to whom *be* glory for ever and ever. Amen.   *2 Timothy 4:18*

We know that whosoever is born of God sinneth not; but he that is begotten of God keepeth himself, and that wicked one toucheth him not.   *1 John 5:18*

Who hath delivered us from the power of darkness, and hath translated *us* into the kingdom of his dear Son.   *Colossians 1:13*

But the Lord is faithful, who shall stablish you, and keep *you* from evil.   *2 Thessalonians 3:3*

For I am persuaded, that neither death, nor life, nor angels, nor principalities, nor powers, nor things present, nor things to come, Nor height, nor depth, nor any other creature, shall be able to separate us from the love of God, which is in Christ Jesus our Lord.

Romans 8:38-39

The angel of the LORD encampeth round about them that fear him, and delivereth them. *Psalm 34:7*

Ye that love the LORD, hate evil: he preserveth the souls of his saints; he delivereth them out of the hand of the wicked. *Psalm 97:10*

Because thou hast made the LORD, *which is* my refuge, *even* the most High, thy habitation; There shall no evil befall thee, neither shall any plague come nigh thy dwelling. For he shall give his angels charge over thee, to keep thee in all thy ways. *Psalm 91:9-11*

Eternal Life

For God so loved the world, that he gave his only begotten Son, that whosoever believeth in him should not perish, but have everlasting life. *John 3:16*

He that believeth on the Son hath everlasting life.   *John 3:36*

These things have I written unto you that believe on the name of the Son of God; that ye may know that ye have eternal life.

1 John 5:13

This is the promise that he hath promised us, *even* eternal life.   *1 John 2:25*

But now being made free from sin, and become servants to God, ye have your fruit unto holiness, and the end everlasting life. For the wages of sin *is* death; but the gift of God is eternal life through Jesus Christ our Lord.

Romans 6:22-23

My sheep hear my voice, and I know them, and they follow me: And I give unto them eternal life; and they shall never perish.

John 10:27-28

In hope of eternal life, which God, that cannot lie, promised before the world began. *Titus 1:2*

He that loveth his life shall lose it; and he that hateth his life in this world shall keep it unto life eternal.   *John 12:25*

Verily, verily, I say unto you, He that heareth my word, and believeth on him that sent me, hath everlasting life, and shall not come into condemnation; but is passed from death unto life. *John 5:24*

And this is the record, that God hath given to us eternal life, and this life is in his Son. He that hath the Son hath life; *and* he that hath not the Son of God hath not life.
1 John 5:11-12

Family Blessings

He blesseth the habitation of the just.
Proverbs 3:33

The house of the righteous shall stand.
Proverbs 12:7

Lo, children *are* an heritage of the LORD: *and* the fruit of the womb *is his* reward.
Psalm 127:3

And I will give them one heart, and one way, that they may fear me for ever, for the good of them, and of their children after them.
Jeremiah 32:39

Observe and hear all these words which I
command thee, that it may go well with thee,
and with thy children after thee for ever,
when thou doest *that which is* good and right
in the sight of the LORD thy God.
                                    Deuteronomy 12:28

The just *man* walketh in his integrity: his
children *are* blessed after him.   *Proverbs 20:7*

For I will pour water upon him that is thirsty,
and floods upon the dry ground: I will pour
my spirit upon thy seed, and my blessing upon
thine offspring.   *Isaiah 44:3*

Blessed *is* the man *that* feareth the LORD, *that*
delighteth greatly in his commandments. His
seed shall be mighty upon earth: the generation of the upright shall be blessed.
                                    Psalm 112:1-2

And all thy children *shall be* taught of the
LORD; and great *shall be* the peace of thy children.   *Isaiah 54:13*

Honor thy father and mother; which is the
first commandment with promise; That it may
be well with thee, and thou mayest live long
on the earth.   *Ephesians 6:2-3*

Thou shalt keep therefore his statutes, and his commandments, which I command thee this day, that it may go well with thee, and with thy children after thee, and that thou mayest prolong *thy* days upon the earth, which the LORD thy God giveth thee, for ever.
Deuteronomy 4:40

Thy wife *shall be* as a fruitful vine by the sides of thine house: thy children like olive plants round about thy table. *Psalm 128:3*

The LORD shall increase you more and more, you and your children. *Psalm 115:14*

Train up a child in the way he should go: and when he is old, he will not depart from it.
Proverbs 22:6

And thou shalt rejoice in every good *thing* which the LORD thy God hath given unto thee, and unto thine house. *Deuteronomy 26:11*

As arrows *are* in the hand of a mighty man; so *are* children of the youth. Happy *is* the man that hath his quiver full of them: they shall not be ashamed, but they shall speak with the enemies in the gate. *Psalm 127:4-5*

On this wise ye shall bless the children of Israel, saying unto them: The LORD bless thee, and keep thee: The LORD make his face shine upon thee, and be gracious unto thee: The LORD lift up his countenance upon thee, and give thee peace. And they shall put my name upon the children of Israel; and I will bless them.   *Numbers 6:23-27*

And if it seem evil unto you to serve the LORD, choose you this day whom ye will serve; whether the gods which your fathers served that *were* on the other side of the flood, or the gods of the Amorites, in whose land ye dwell: but as for me and my house, we will serve the LORD.   *Joshua 24:15*

And he shall turn the heart of the fathers to the children, and the heart of the children to their fathers, lest I come and smite the earth with a curse.   *Malachi 4:6*

And they said, Believe on the Lord Jesus Christ, and thou shalt be saved, and thy house.
                                                 Acts 16:31

A good *man* leaveth an inheritance to his children's children: and the wealth of the sinner *is* laid up for the just.   *Proverbs 13:22*

Correct thy son, and he shall give thee rest; yea, he shall give delight unto thy soul.

Proverbs 29:17

The father of the righteous shall greatly rejoice: and he that begetteth a wise *child* shall have joy of him. *Proverbs 23:24*

Who can find a virtuous woman? for her price *is* far above rubies. The heart of her husband doth safely trust in her, so that he shall have no need of spoil...Her children arise up, and call her blessed; her husband *also,* and he praiseth her. *Proverbs 31:10-11, 28*

Children's children *are* the crown of old men; and the glory of children *are* their fathers.

Proverbs 17:6

Favor

Of a truth I perceive that God is no respecter of persons: But in every nation he that feareth him, and worketh righteousness, is accepted with him. *Acts 10:34-35*

But the LORD was with Joseph, and showed him mercy, and gave him favor in the sight of the keeper of the prison. *Genesis 39:21*

And I will give this people favor in the sight of
the Egyptians: and it shall come to pass, that,
when ye go, ye shall not go empty.

Exodus 3:21

And the LORD gave the people favor in the
sight of the Egyptians, so that they lent unto
them *such things as they required.* And they
spoiled the Egyptians.   *Exodus 12:36*

O Naphtali, satisfied with favor, and full with
the blessing of the LORD: possess thou the
west and the south.   *Deuteronomy 33:23*

Then she said, Let me find favor in thy sight,
my lord; for that thou hast comforted me, and
for that thou hast spoken friendly unto thine
handmaid, though I be not like unto one of
thine handmaidens.   *Ruth 2:13*

For they got not the land in possession by
their own sword, neither did their own arm
save them: but thy right hand, and thine arm,
and the light of thy countenance, because
thou hadst a favor unto them.   *Psalm 44:3*

And the child Samuel grew on, and was in favor both with the LORD, and also with men.

1 Samuel 2:26

Thou hast granted me life and favor, and thy visitation hath preserved my spirit.   *Job 10:12*

He shall pray unto God, and he will be favorable unto him: and he shall see his face with joy: for he will render unto man his righteousness.   *Job 33:26*

For thou, LORD, wilt bless the righteous; with favor wilt thou compass him as *with* a shield.
Psalm 5:12

But thou, O LORD, be merciful unto me, and raise me up, that I may requite them. By this I know that thou favorest me, because mine enemy doth not triumph over me And as for me, thou upholdest me in mine integrity, and settest me before thy face for ever.
Psalm 41:10-12

He that diligently seeketh good procureth favor.   *Proverbs 11:27*

A good *man* obtaineth favor of the LORD.
Proverbs 12:2

For his anger *endureth but* a moment; in his favor *is* life: weeping may endure for a night, but joy *cometh* in the morning.   *Psalm 30:5*

For thou *art* the glory of their strength: and in thy favor our horn [power] shall be exalted.
Psalm 89:17

Remember me, O LORD, with the favor *that thou bearest unto* thy people: O visit me with thy salvation.   *Psalm 106:4*

I entreated thy favor with *my* whole heart: be merciful unto me according to thy word.
Psalm 119:58

My son, forget not my law; but let thine heart keep my commandments...So shalt thou find favor and good understanding in the sight of God and man.   *Proverbs 3:1, 4*

For whoso findeth me findeth life, and shall obtain favor of the LORD.   *Proverbs 8:35*

Good understanding giveth favor.
Proverbs 13:15

Among the righteous *there is* favor.
Proverbs 14:9

In the light of the king's countenance *is* life; and his favor *is* as a cloud of the latter rain.
Proverbs 16:15

The king's favor *is* toward a wise servant.
Proverbs 14:35

Whoso findeth a wife findeth a good *thing,* and obtaineth favor of the LORD.   *Proverbs 18:22*

A *good* name *is* rather to be chosen than great riches, *and* loving favor rather than silver and gold.   *Proverbs 22:1*

Children in whom *was* no blemish, but well favored, and skillful in all wisdom, and cunning in knowledge, and understanding science, and such as *had* ability in them to stand in the king's palace, and whom they might teach the learning and the tongue of the Chaldeans.   *Daniel 1:4*

And the patriarchs, moved with envy, sold Joseph into Egypt: but God was with him, And delivered him out of all his afflictions, and gave him favor and wisdom in the sight of Pharaoh king of Egypt; and he made him governor over Egypt and all his house.
Acts 7:9-10

Now God had brought Daniel into favor and tender love with the prince of the eunuchs.
Daniel 1:9

Then was I in his eyes as one that found favor.
Song of Solomon 8:10

In my favor have I had mercy on thee.
Isaiah 60:10

And the angel came in unto her, and said, Hail,
thou that art highly favored, the Lord *is* with
thee: blessed *art* thou among women... And the
angel said unto her, Fear not, Mary: for thou
hast found favor with God.   *Luke 1:28, 30*

And Jesus increased in wisdom and stature,
and in favor with God and man.   *Luke 2:52*

And they, continuing daily with one accord in
the temple, and breaking bread from house to
house, did eat their meat with gladness and
singleness of heart, Praising God, and having
favor with all the people.   *Acts 2:46-47*

Food

Honor the LORD with thy substance, and with
the firstfruits of all thine increase: So shall
thy barns be filled with plenty, and thy
presses shall burst out with new wine.

Proverbs 3:9-10

He hath given meat unto them that fear him: he will ever be mindful of his covenant.

Psalm 111:5

The God of Jacob...Which made heaven, and earth, the sea, and all that therein *is:* which keepeth truth for ever: Which executeth judgment for the oppressed: which giveth food to the hungry. *Psalm 146:5-7*

I have been young, and *now* am old; yet have I not seen the righteous forsaken, nor his seed begging bread. *Psalm 37:25*

Therefore I say unto you, Take no thought for your life, what ye shall eat, or what ye shall drink...Is not the life more than meat...? Behold the fowls of the air: for they sow not, neither do they reap, nor gather into barns; yet your heavenly Father feedeth them. Are ye not much better than they?...Therefore take no thought, saying, What shall we eat? or, What shall we drink?...for your heavenly Father knoweth that ye have need of all these things. But seek ye first the kingdom of God, and his righteousness; and all these things shall be added unto you.

Matthew 6: 25-26, 31-33

The LORD knoweth the days of the upright: and their inheritance shall be for ever. They shall not be ashamed in the evil time: and in the days of famine they shall be satisfied.

Psalm 37:18-19

For by them judgeth he the people; he giveth meat in abundance.   *Job 36:31*

If ye be willing and obedient, ye shall eat the good of the land.   *Isaiah 1:19*

Forgiveness

Blessed *is he whose* transgression *is* forgiven, *whose* sin *is* covered. Blessed *is* the man unto whom the LORD imputeth not iniquity, and in whose spirit *there is* no guile.   *Psalm 32:1-2*

If we confess our sins, he is faithful and just to forgive us *our* sins, and to cleanse us from all unrighteousness.   *1 John 1:9*

Who hath delivered us from the power of darkness, and hath translated *us* into the kingdom of his dear Son: In whom we have redemption through his blood, *even* the forgiveness of sins.   *Colossians 1:14*

I, *even* I, *am* he that blotteth out thy transgressions for mine own sake, and will not remember thy sins.   *Isaiah 43:25*

As far as the east is from the west, *so* far hath he removed our transgressions from us.
                                        Psalm 103:12

I write unto you, little children, because your sins are forgiven you for his name's sake.
                                        1 John 2:12

In whom we have redemption through his blood, the forgiveness of sins, according to the riches of his grace.   *Ephesians 1:7*

Come now, and let us reason together, saith the LORD: though your sins be as scarlet, they shall be as white as snow; though they be red like crimson, they shall be as wool.   *Isaiah 1:18*

And you, being dead in your sins and the uncircumcision of your flesh, hath he quickened together with him, having forgiven you all trespasses.   *Colossians 2:13*

To him give all the prophets witness, that through his name whosoever believeth in him shall receive remission of sins.   *Acts 10:43*

But *there is* forgiveness with thee, that thou mayest be feared.   *Psalm 130:4*

There is therefore now no condemnation to them which are in Christ Jesus, who walk not after the flesh, but after the Spirit.
Romans 8:1

Thou hast forgiven the iniquity of thy people, thou hast covered all their sin.   *Psalm 85:2*

If my people, which are called by my name, shall humble themselves, and pray, and seek my face, and turn from their wicked ways; then will I hear from heaven, and will forgive their sin, and will heal their land.
2 Chronicles 7:14

And I will cleanse them from all their iniquity, whereby they have sinned against me; and I will pardon all their iniquities, whereby they have sinned, and whereby they have transgressed against me.   *Jeremiah 33:8*

I will put my law in their inward parts, and write it in their hearts; and will be their God, and they shall be my people...For I will forgive their iniquity, and I will remember their sin no more.   *Jeremiah 31:33-34*

Freedom

If the Son therefore shall make you free, ye shall be free indeed. *John 8:36*

For sin shall not have dominion over you: for ye are not under the law, but under grace.
Romans 6:14

There is therefore now no condemnation to them which are in Christ Jesus, who walk not after the flesh, but after the Spirit. For the law of the Spirit of life in Christ Jesus hath made me free from the law of sin and death.
Romans 8:2

Stand fast therefore in the liberty wherewith Christ hath made us free, and be not entangled again with the yoke of bondage.
Galatians 5:1

But now being made free from sin, and become servants to God, ye have your fruit unto holiness, and the end everlasting life.
Romans 6:22

Now the Lord is that Spirit: and where the Spirit of the Lord *is,* there *is* liberty.
2 Corinthians 3:17

The spirit of the Lord GOD *is* upon me...he hath sent me to bind up the brokenhearted, to proclaim liberty to the captives, and the opening of the prison to *them that are* bound.

Isaiah 61:1

God's Presence

Fear not: for I am with thee.   *Isaiah 43:5*

And he said, My presence shall go *with thee*, and I will give thee rest.   *Exodus 33:14*

Yea, though I walk through the valley of the shadow of death, I will fear no evil: for thou *art* with me.   *Psalm 23:4*

Surely the righteous shall give thanks unto thy name: the upright shall dwell in thy presence.   *Psalm 140:13*

Thou shalt hide them in the secret of thy presence.   *Psalm 31:20*

If ye love me, keep my commandments. And I will pray the Father, and he shall give you another Comforter, that he may abide with you for ever.   *John 14:15-16*

Thou wilt show me the path of life: in thy presence *is* fullness of joy.   *Psalm 16:11*

For where two or three are gathered together in my name, there am I in the midst of them.
                                        Matthew 18:20

Draw nigh to God, and he will draw nigh to you.   *James 4:8*

Behold, I stand at the door, and knock: if any man hear my voice, and open the door, I will come in to him, and will sup with him, and he with me.   *Revelation 3:20*

And, lo, I am with you alway, *even* unto the end of the world.   *Matthew 28:20*

God's Spirit

And it shall come to pass afterward, *that* I will pour out my spirit upon all flesh; and your sons and your daughters shall prophesy, your old men shall dream dreams, your young men shall see visions. And also upon the servants and upon the handmaids in those days will I pour out my spirit.   *Joel 2:28-29*

Behold, I will pour out my spirit unto you, I will make known my words unto you.
Proverbs 1:23

Hereby know we that we dwell in him, and he in us, because he hath given us of his Spirit.
1 John 4:13

For I will pour water upon him that is thirsty, and floods upon the dry ground: I will pour my spirit upon thy seed, and my blessing upon thine offspring.   *Isaiah 44:3*

If ye then, being evil, know how to give good gifts unto your children: how much more shall *your* heavenly Father give the Holy Spirit to them that ask him?   *Luke 11:13*

Nevertheless I tell you the truth; It is expedient for you that I go away: for if I go not away, the Comforter will not come unto you; but if I depart, I will send him unto you.   *John 16:7*

And I will pray the Father, and he shall give you another Comforter, that he may abide with you for ever; *Even* the Spirit of truth...ye know him; for he dwelleth with you, and shall be in you.   *John 14:16-17*

But when the Comforter is come, whom I will send unto you from the Father, *even* the Spirit of truth, which proceedeth from the Father, he shall testify of me. *John 15:26*

Because ye are sons, God hath sent forth the Spirit of his Son into your hearts, crying, Abba, Father. *Galatians 4:6*

I [John the Baptist] indeed baptize you with water unto repentance: but he that cometh after me is mightier than I, whose shoes I am not worthy to bear: he shall baptize you with the Holy Ghost, and *with* fire.

Matthew 3:11

Then Peter said unto them, Repent, and be baptized every one of you in the name of Jesus Christ for the remission of sins, and ye shall receive the gift of the Holy Ghost. For the promise is unto you, and to your children, and to all that are afar off, *even* as many as the Lord our God shall call. *Acts 2:38-39*

But ye shall receive power, after that the Holy Ghost is come upon you: and ye shall be witnesses unto me...unto the uttermost part of the earth. *Acts 1:8*

God's Word

For the word of God *is* quick, and powerful, and sharper than any two-edged sword, piercing even to the dividing asunder of soul and spirit, and of the joints and marrow, and *is* a discerner of the thoughts and intents of the heart.   *Hebrews 4:12*

The grass withereth, the flower fadeth: but the word of our God shall stand for ever. *Isaiah 40:8*

Thy word *is* a lamp unto my feet, and a light unto my path.   *Psalm 119:105*

And now, brethren, I commend you to God, and to the word of his grace, which is able to build you up, and to give you an inheritance among all them which are sanctified.   *Acts 20:32*

The secret *things belong* unto the LORD our God: but those *things which are* revealed *belong* unto us and to our children for ever, that *we* may do all the words of this law.

Deuteronomy 29:29

Be ye mindful always of his covenant; the word *which* he commanded to a thousand generations.   *1 Chronicles 16:15*

It is written, Man shall not live by bread alone, but by every word that proceedeth out of the mouth of God. *Matthew 4:4*

Search the Scriptures; for in them ye think ye have eternal life: and they are they which testify of me. *John 5:39*

So shall my word be that goeth forth out of my mouth: it shall not return unto me void, but it shall accomplish that which I please, and it shall prosper *in the thing* whereto I sent it. *Isaiah 55:11*

All Scripture *is* given by inspiration of God, and *is* profitable for doctrine, for reproof, for correction, for instruction in righteousness: That the man of God may be perfect, thoroughly furnished unto all good works. *2 Timothy 3:16-17*

Being born again, not of corruptible seed, but of incorruptible, by the word of God, which liveth and abideth for ever...But the word of the Lord endureth for ever. And this is the word which by the gospel is preached unto you. *1 Peter 1:23, 25*

For ever, O LORD, thy word is settled in heaven. *Psalm 119:89*

Guidance

Show me thy ways, O LORD; teach me thy
paths. Lead me in thy truth, and teach me: for
thou *art* the God of my salvation; on thee do I
wait all the day...The meek will he guide in
judgment: and the meek will he teach his way.
All the paths of the LORD *are* mercy and truth
unto such as keep his covenant and his testimonies.   *Psalm 25:4-5, 9-10*

For thou *art* my rock and my fortress; therefore for thy name's sake lead me, and guide
me.   *Psalm 31:3*

The steps of a *good* man are ordered by the
LORD: and he delighteth in his way.
                                       Psalm 37:23

I will instruct thee and teach thee in the way
which thou shalt go: I will guide thee with
mine eye.   *Psalm 32:8*
He keepeth the paths of judgment, and preserveth the way of his saints.   *Proverbs 2:8*

Trust in the LORD with all thine heart; and
lean not unto thine own understanding. In all
thy ways acknowledge him, and he shall direct
thy paths.   *Proverbs 3:5-6*

God *is* our God for ever and ever: he will be our guide *even* unto death.   *Psalm 48:14*

Thine ear shall hear a word behind thee, saying, This *is* the way, walk ye in it, when ye turn to the right hand. and when ye turn to the left.   *Isaiah 30:21*

My son, keep thy father's commandment, and forsake not the law of thy mother: Bind them continually upon thine heart, *and* tie them about thy neck. When thou goest, it shall lead thee; when thou sleepest, it shall keep thee; and *when* thou awakest, it shall talk with thee. For the commandment *is* a lamp; and the law *is* light; and reproofs of instruction *are* the way of life.   *Proverbs 6:20-23*

And the LORD shall guide thee continually, and satisfy thy soul in drought, and make fat thy bones: and thou shalt be like a watered garden, and like a spring of water, whose waters fail not.   *Isaiah 58:11*

They shall not hunger nor thirst; neither shall the heat nor sun smite them: for he that hath mercy on them shall lead them, even by the springs of water shall he guide them.
     Isaiah 49:10

The LORD *is* my shepherd...he leadeth me in the paths of righteousness for his name's sake.
Psalm 23:1, 3

If I take the wings of the morning, *and* dwell in the uttermost parts of the sea; Even there shall thy hand lead me, and thy right hand shall hold me. *Psalm 139:9-10*

Thou shalt guide me with thy counsel, and afterward receive me *to* glory. *Psalm 73:24*

He shall feed his flock like a shepherd: he shall gather the lambs with his arm, and carry *them* in his bosom, *and* shall gently lead those that are with young. *Isaiah 40:11*

And I will bring the blind by a way *that* they knew not; I will lead them in paths *that* they have not known: I will make darkness light before them, and crooked things straight. These things will I do unto them, and not forsake them. *Isaiah 42:16*

Through the tender mercy of our God; whereby the dayspring from on high hath visited us, To give light to them that sit in darkness and *in* the shadow of death, to guide our feet into the way of peace. *Luke 1:78-79*

Howbeit when he, the Spirit of truth, is come, he will guide you into all truth: for he shall not speak of himself; but whatsoever he shall hear, *that* shall he speak: and he will show you things to come.   *John 16:13*

I lead in the way of righteousness, in the midst of the paths of judgment: That I may cause those that love me to inherit substance; and I will fill their treasures. *Proverbs 8:20-21*

Harvest

When thou cuttest down thine harvest in thy field, and hast forgot a sheaf in the field, thou shalt not go again to fetch it: it shall be for the stranger, for the fatherless, and for the widow: that the LORD thy God may bless thee in all the work of thine hands.   *Deuteronomy 24:19*

If ye hearken to these judgments, and keep, and do them, that the LORD thy God shall keep unto thee the covenant...he will also bless the fruit of thy womb, and the fruit of thy land, thy corn, and thy wine, and thine oil, the increase of thy kine, and the flocks of thy sheep, in the land which he sware unto thy fathers to give thee.   *Deuteronomy 7:12-13*

While the earth remaineth, seedtime and harvest, and cold and heat, and summer and winter, and day and night shall not cease.
Genesis 8:22

If ye walk in my statutes, and keep my commandments, and do them; Then I will give you rain in due season, and the land shall yield her increase, and the trees of the field shall yield their fruit. And your threshing shall reach unto the vintage, and the vintage shall reach unto the sowing time: and ye shall eat your bread to the full, and dwell in your land safely.
Leviticus 26:3-5

Let us now fear the LORD our God, that giveth rain, both the former and the latter, in his season: he reserveth unto us the appointed weeks of the harvest.
Jeremiah 5:24

Ask ye of the LORD rain in the time of the latter rain; *so* the LORD shall make bright clouds, and give them showers of rain, to every one grass in the field.
Zechariah 10:1

He causeth the grass to grow for the cattle, and herb for the service of man: that he may bring forth food out of the earth.
Psalm 104:14

Also, O Judah, he hath set an harvest for thee.
Hosea 6:11

Then shall he give the rain of thy seed, that
thou shalt sow the ground withal; and bread
of the increase of the earth, and it shall be fat
and plenteous: in that day shall thy cattle feed
in large pastures.   *Isaiah 30:23*

Then saith he unto his disciples, The harvest
truly *is* plenteous, but the laborers *are* few;
Pray ye therefore the Lord of the harvest, that
he will send forth laborers into his harvest.
Matthew 9:37-38

Healing

I *am* the LORD that healeth thee.
Exodus 15:26

And he received them, and spake unto them of
the kingdom of God, and healed them that
had need of healing.   *Luke 9:11*

He *was* wounded for our transgressions, *he
was* bruised for our iniquities: the chastise-
ment of our peace *was* upon him; and with his
stripes we are healed.   *Isaiah 53:5*

Bless the LORD, O my soul, and forget not all his benefits, Who forgiveth all thine iniquities; who healeth all thy diseases.

Psalm 103:2-3

And Jesus went about all Galilee, teaching in their synagogues, and preaching the gospel of the kingdom, and healing all manner of sickness and all manner of disease among the people.   *Matthew 4:23*

Who his own self bare our sins in his own body on the tree, that we, being dead to sins, should live unto righteousness: by whose stripes ye were healed.   *1 Peter 2:24*

Confess *your* faults one to another, and pray one for another, that ye may be healed. The effectual fervent prayer of a righteous man availeth much.   *James 5:16*

Heal me, O LORD, and I shall be healed; save me, and I shall be saved: for thou *art* my praise.   *Jeremiah 17:14*

But unto you that fear my name shall the Sun of righteousness arise with healing in his wings.   *Malachi 4:2*

Health

Wherefore it shall come to pass, if ye hearken to these judgments, and keep, and do them...the LORD will take away from thee all sickness, and will put none of the evil diseases of Egypt...upon thee. *Deuteronomy 7:12, 15*

Fear the LORD, and depart from evil. It shall be health to thy navel, and marrow to thy bones. *Proverbs 3:7-8*

God be merciful unto us, and bless us; *and* cause his face to shine upon us; That thy way may be known upon earth, thy saving health among all nations. *Psalm 67:1-2*

For I will restore health unto thee, and I will heal thee of thy wounds, saith the LORD. *Jeremiah 30:17*

Then shall thy light break forth as the morning, and thine health shall spring forth speedily: and thy righteousness shall go before thee; the glory of the LORD shall be thy reward. *Isaiah 58:8*

There shall no evil befall thee, neither shall any plague come nigh thy dwelling. *Psalm 91:10*

Behold, I will bring it health and cure, and I will cure them.   *Jeremiah 33:6*

Beloved, I wish above all things that thou mayest prosper and be in health, even as thy soul prospereth.   *3 John 1:2*

Heaven

Nevertheless we, according to his promise, look for new heavens and a new earth, wherein dwelleth righteousness.   *2 Peter 3:13*

And Jesus said unto him, Verily I say unto thee, Today shalt thou be with me in paradise.
                                    Luke 23:43

Rejoice, and be exceeding glad: for great *is* your reward in heaven.   *Matthew 5:12*

And I John saw the holy city, new Jerusalem, coming down from God out of heaven, prepared as a bride adorned for her husband. And I heard a great voice out of heaven saying, Behold, the tabernacle of God *is* with men, and he will dwell with them, and they shall be his people, and God himself shall be with them, *and be* their God.   *Revelation 21:3*

For here have we no continuing city, but we
seek one to come. *Hebrews 13:14*

To an inheritance incorruptible, and undefiled, and that fadeth not away, reserved in
heaven for you, Who are kept by the power of
God through faith unto salvation ready to be
revealed in the last time. *1 Peter 1:4-5*

Wherefore the rather, brethren, give diligence
to make your calling and election sure: for if
ye do these things, ye shall never fall: For so
an entrance shall be ministered unto you
abundantly into the everlasting kingdom of
our Lord and Savior Jesus Christ.
2 Peter 1:10-11

For the hope which is laid up for you in
heaven. *Colossians 1:5*

Honor

Now the LORD saith, Be it far from me; for
them that honor me I will honor.
1 Samuel 2:30

A gracious woman retaineth honor: and
strong *men* retain riches. *Proverbs 11:16*

But glory, honor, and peace, to every man that
worketh good, to the Jew first, and also to the
Gentile: For there is no respect of persons
with God.   *Romans 2:10-11*

And the LORD hath avouched thee this day to
be his peculiar people, as he hath promised
thee, and that *thou* shouldest keep all his
commandments; And to make thee high above
all nations which he hath made, in praise, and
in name, and in honor; and that thou mayest
be an holy people unto the LORD thy God, as
he hath spoken.   *Deuteronomy 26:18-19*

If any man serve me, let him follow me; and
where I am, there shall also my servant be: if
any man serve me, him will *my* Father honor.
                                    John 12:26

Happy *is* the man *that* findeth wisdom, and
the man *that* getteth understanding...Length
of days *is* in her right hand; *and* in her left
hand riches and honor.   *Proverbs 3:13, 16*

What is man, that thou art mindful of him?
and the son of man, that thou visitest him?
For thou hast made him a little lower than
the angels, and hast crowned him with glory
and honor.   *Psalm 8:4-5*

Because he hath set his love upon me, therefore will I deliver him: I will set him on high,
because he hath known my name. He shall
call upon me, and I will answer him: I *will be*
with him in trouble; I will deliver him, and
honor him.   *Psalm 91:14-15*

And God said to Solomon, Because this was in
thine heart, and thou hast not asked riches,
wealth, or honor, nor the life of thine enemies,
neither yet hast asked long life; but hast asked
wisdom and knowledge for thyself, that thou
mayest judge my people, over whom I have
made thee king: Wisdom and knowledge *is*
granted unto thee; and I will give thee riches,
and wealth, and honor.   *2 Chronicles 1:11-12*

Wisdom *is* the principal thing; *therefore* get
wisdom: and with all thy getting get understanding. Exalt her, and she shall promote
thee: she shall bring thee to honor, when thou
dost embrace her.   *Proverbs 4:7-8*

I wisdom dwell with prudence, and find out
knowledge of witty inventions...I love them
that love me; and those that seek me early
shall find me. Riches and honor *are* with me;
yea, durable riches and righteousness.
                                    Proverbs 8:12, 17-18

The fear of the LORD *is* the instruction of wisdom; and before honor *is* humility.
Proverbs 15:33

Blessed *is* the man *that* feareth the LORD, ...His horn shall be exalted with honor.
Psalm 112:1, 9

He that followeth after righteousness and mercy findeth life, righteousness, and honor.
Proverbs 21:21

A man's pride shall bring him low: but honor shall uphold the humble in spirit. *Proverbs 29:23*

Who can find a virtuous woman? for her price *is* far above rubies...Strength and honor *are* her clothing; and she shall rejoice in time to come.   *Proverbs 31:10, 25*

Poverty and shame *shall be to* him that refuseth instruction: but he that regardeth reproof shall be honored.   *Proverbs 13:18*

Hope

Christ in you, the hope of glory.
Colossians 1:27

The eyes of your understanding being enlightened; that ye may know what is the hope of his calling, and what the riches of the glory of his inheritance in the saints.   *Ephesians 1:18*

Now the God of hope fill you with all joy and peace in believing, that ye may abound in hope, through the power of the Holy Ghost.
Romans 15:13

For thou *art* my hope, O Lord GOD: *thou art* my trust from my youth.   *Psalm 71:5*

For the hope which is laid up for you in heaven, whereof ye heard before in the word of the truth of the gospel.   *Colossians 1:5*

That by two immutable things, in which *it was* impossible for God to lie, we might have a strong consolation, who have fled for refuge to lay hold upon the hope set before us: Which *hope* we have as an anchor of the soul, both sure and stedfast, and which entereth into that within the veil.   *Hebrews 6:18-19*

For whatsoever things were written aforetime were written for our learning, that we through patience and comfort of the scriptures might have hope.   *Romans 15:4*

By whom also we...rejoice in hope of the glory
of God. And hope maketh not ashamed; because the love of God is shed abroad in our
hearts by the Holy Ghost which is given unto
us.   *Romans 5:2, 5*

Be of good courage, and he shall strengthen
your heart, all ye that hope in the LORD.
                                       Psalm 31:24

Blessed *be* the God and Father of our Lord Jesus Christ, which according to his abundant
mercy hath begotten us again unto a lively
hope by the resurrection of Jesus Christ from
the dead.   *1 Peter 1:3*

Instruction

He that refuseth instruction despiseth his
own soul: but he that heareth reproof getteth
understanding. The fear of the LORD *is* the
instruction of wisdom, and before honor *is*
humility.   *Proverbs 15:32-33*

For his God doth instruct him to discretion,
and doth teach him...This also cometh forth
from the LORD of hosts, *which* is wonderful in
counsel.   *Isaiah 28:26, 29*

I will instruct thee and teach thee in the way which thou shalt go: I will guide thee with mine eye.   *Psalm 32:8*

What man *is* he that feareth the LORD? him shall he teach in the way *that* he shall choose.
                    Psalm 25:12

Receive my instruction, and not silver; and knowledge rather than choice gold. For wisdom *is* better than rubies; and all the things that may be desired are not to be compared to it...Counsel *is* mine, and sound wisdom: I *am* understanding; I have strength.
                    Proverbs 8:10-11, 14

All scripture is given by inspiration of God, and is profitable for doctrine, for reproof, for correction, for instruction in righteousness: That the man of God may be perfect, thoroughly furnished unto all good works.
                    2 Timothy 3:16-17

Hear instruction, and be wise, and refuse it not. Blessed *is* the man that heareth me, watching daily at my gates, waiting at the posts of my doors. For whoso findeth me findeth life, and shall obtain favor of the LORD.
                    Proverbs 8:33-35

To know wisdom and instruction; to perceive the words of understanding; To receive the instruction of wisdom, justice, and judgment, and equity; To give subtlety to the simple, to the young man knowledge and discretion; A wise *man* will hear, and will increase learning; and a man of understanding shall attain unto wise counsels.   *Proverbs 1:2-5*

Hear counsel, and receive instruction, that thou mayest be wise in thy latter end. *There are* many devices in a man's heart; nevertheless the counsel of the LORD, that shall stand.
                                      Proverbs 19:20-21

Take fast hold of instruction; let *her* not go: keep her; for she *is* thy life.   *Proverbs 4:13*

The fear of the LORD *is* the beginning of knowledge: *but* fools despise wisdom and instruction. My son, hear the instruction of thy father, and forsake not the law of thy mother: For they *shall be* an ornament of grace unto thy head, and chains about thy neck.
                                      Proverbs 1:7-9

The counsel of the LORD standeth for ever, the thoughts of his heart to all generations.
                                      Psalm 33:11

Good and upright *is* the LORD: therefore will he teach sinners in the way. The meek will he guide in judgment and...will he teach his way.
Psalm 25:8-9

Give *instruction* to a wise *man,* and he will be yet wiser: teach a just *man,* and he will increase in learning. The fear of the LORD *is* the beginning of wisdom: and the knowledge of the holy *is* understanding.   *Proverbs 9:9-10*

Understanding *is* a wellspring of life unto him that hath it: but the instruction of fools *is* folly. The heart of the wise teacheth his mouth, and addeth learning to his lips.
Proverbs 16:22-23

Come ye, and let us go up to the mountain of the LORD, to the house of the God of Jacob; and he will teach us of his ways, and we will walk in his paths: for out of Zion shall go forth the law, and the word of the LORD from Jerusalem.   *Isaiah 2:3*

But the Comforter, *which is* the Holy Ghost, whom the Father will send in my name, he shall teach you all things, and bring all things to your remembrance, whatsoever I have said unto you.   *John 14:26*

But the anointing which ye have received of
him abideth in you, and ye need not that any
man teach you: but as the same anointing
teacheth you of all things, and is truth, and is
no lie, and even as it hath taught you, ye shall
abide in him.   *1 John 2:27*

Thou shalt guide me with thy counsel, and
afterward receive me *to* glory.   *Psalm 73:24*

Jesus' Return

For the Lord himself shall descend from
heaven with a shout, with the voice of the
archangel, and with the trump of God: and
the dead in Christ shall rise first: Then we
which are alive *and* remain shall be caught up
together with them in the clouds, to meet the
Lord in the air: and so shall we ever be with
the Lord.   *1 Thessalonians 4:16-17*

Looking for that blessed hope, and the glorious appearing of the great God and our Savior
Jesus Christ.   *Titus 2:13*

Unto them that look for him shall he appear
the second time without sin unto salvation.
                                       Hebrews 9:28

In my Father's house are many mansions: if *it were* not so, I would have told you. I go to prepare a place for you. And if I go and prepare a place for you, I will come again, and receive you unto myself; that where I am, *there* ye may also be. *John 14:2-3*

Behold, he cometh with clouds; and every eye shall see him. *Revelation 1:7*

For as the lightning cometh out of the east, and shineth even unto the west; so shall also the coming of the Son of man be...And then shall appear the sign of the Son of man in heaven: and then shall all the tribes of the earth mourn, and they shall see the Son of man coming in the clouds of heaven with power and great glory. *Matthew 24:27, 30*

When Christ, *who is* our life, shall appear, then shall ye also appear with him in glory.
Colossians 3:4

For I know *that* my redeemer liveth, and *that* he shall stand at the latter *day* upon the earth. *Job 19:25*

Blessed *are* those servants, whom the lord when he cometh shall find watching. *Luke 12:37*

But we know that, when he shall appear, we shall be like him; for we shall see him as he is.
1 John 3:2

For as often as ye eat this bread, and drink this cup, ye do show the Lord's death till he come.   *1 Corinthians 11:26*

Ye have heard how I said unto you, I said unto you, I go away, and come *again* unto you. If ye loved me, ye would rejoice, because I said, I go unto the Father.   *John 14:28*

And Jesus said, I am: and ye shall see the Son of man sitting on the right hand of power, and coming in the clouds of heaven.   *Mark 14:62*

This same Jesus, which is taken up from you into heaven, shall so come in like manner as ye have seen him go into heaven.   *Acts 1:11*

Joy

They that sow in tears shall reap in joy. He that goeth forth and weepeth, bearing precious seed, shall doubtless come again with rejoicing, bringing his sheaves *with him*.

Psalm 126:5-6

And the ransomed of the LORD shall return, and come to Zion with songs and everlasting joy upon their heads: they shall obtain joy and gladness, and sorrow and sighing shall flee away .   *Isaiah 35:10*

Thou wilt show me the path of life: in thy presence *is* fullness of joy; at thy right hand *there are* pleasures for evermore. *Psalm 16:11*

Whom having not seen, ye love; in whom, though now ye see *him* not, yet believing, ye rejoice with joy unspeakable and full of glory.
1 Peter 1:8

These things have I spoken unto you, that my joy might remain in you, and *that* your joy might be full.   *John 15:11*

The LORD thy God in the midst of thee *is* mighty; he will save, he will rejoice over thee with joy; he will rest in his love, he will joy over thee with singing.   *Zephaniah 3:17*

For ye shall go out with joy, and be led forth with peace: the mountains and the hills shall break forth before you into singing, and all the trees of the field shall clap *their* hands.
Isaiah 55:12

And the angel said unto them, Fear not: for, behold, I bring you good tidings of great joy, which shall be to all people.   *Luke 2:10*

For the kingdom of God is not meat and drink; but righteousness, and peace, and joy in the Holy Ghost.   *Romans 14:17*

For *God* giveth to a man that *is* good in his sight wisdom, and knowledge, and joy.
                                         Ecclesiastes 2:26

Go your way, eat the fat, and drink the sweet, and send portions unto them for whom nothing is prepared: for *this* day *is* holy unto our Lord: neither be ye sorry; for the joy of the LORD is your strength.   *Nehemiah 8:10*

I will greatly rejoice in the LORD, my soul shall be joyful in my God; for he hath clothed me with the garments of salvation, he hath covered me with the robe of righteousness, as a bridegroom decketh *himself* with ornaments, and as a bride adorneth *herself* with her jewels.   *Isaiah 61:10*

I will see you again, and your heart shall rejoice, and your joy no man taketh from you.
                                         John 16:22

Yet I will rejoice in the LORD, I will joy in the God of my salvation.   *Habakkuk 3:18*

Life after Death

But if the Spirit of him that raised up Jesus from the dead dwell in you, he that raised up Christ from the dead shall also quicken your mortal bodies by his Spirit that dwelleth in you.   *Romans 8:11*

Jesus said unto her, I am the resurrection, and the life: he that believeth in me, though he were dead, yet shall he live: And whosoever liveth and believeth in me shall never die.
     John 11:25-26

For if we believe that Jesus died and rose again, even so them also which sleep in Jesus will God bring with him.
     1 Thessalonians 4:14

In a moment, in the twinkling of an eye, at the last trump: for the trumpet shall sound, and the dead shall be raised incorruptible, and we shall be changed. For this corruptible must put on incorruption, and this mortal *must* put on immortality.   *1 Corinthians 15:52-53*

Knowing that he which raised up the Lord Jesus shall raise up us also by Jesus, and shall present *us* with you.   *2 Corinthians 4:14*

Therefore are they before the throne of God, and serve him day and night in his temple: and he that sitteth on the throne shall dwell among them. They shall hunger no more, neither thirst any more; neither shall the sun light on them, nor any heat. For the Lamb which is in the midst of the throne shall feed them, and shall lead them unto living fountains of waters: and God shall wipe away all tears from their eyes.   *Revelation 7:15-17*

Longevity

The fear of the LORD prolongeth days: but the years of the wicked shall be shortened.

Proverbs 10:27

Because he hath set his love upon me...With long life will I satisfy him, and show him my salvation.   *Psalm 91:14, 16*

Forget not my law; but let thine heart keep my commandments: For length of days, and long life, and peace, shall they add to thee.

Proverbs 3:1-2

The fear of the LORD *is* the beginning of wisdom...For by me thy days shall be multiplied, and the years of thy life shall be increased.
Proverbs 9:10-11

Exalt her [wisdom], and she shall promote thee...and the years of thy life shall be many.
Proverbs 4:8, 10

That thou mightest fear the LORD thy God, to keep all his statutes and his commandments, which I command thee, thou, and thy son, and thy son's son, all the days of thy life; and that thy days may be prolonged. *Deuteronomy 6:2*

Ye shall walk in all the ways which the LORD your God hath commanded you, that ye may live, and *that it may be* well with you, and *that* ye may prolong *your* days in the land which ye shall possess. *Deuteronomy 5:33*

Honor thy father and thy mother: that thy days may be long upon the land which the LORD thy God giveth thee. *Exodus 20:12*

Honor thy father and mother; which is the first commandment with promise; That it may be well with thee, and thou mayest live long on the earth. *Ephesians 6:2-3*

Love

For God so loved the world, that he gave his only begotten Son, that whosoever believeth in him should not perish, but have everlasting life.   *John 3:16*

The LORD hath appeared of old unto me, *saying,* Yea, I have loved thee with an everlasting love: therefore with lovingkindness have I drawn thee.   *Jeremiah 31:3*

As the Father hath loved me, so have I loved you: continue ye in my love.   *John 15:9*

Behold, what manner of love the Father hath bestowed upon us, that we should be called the sons of God: therefore the world knoweth us not, because it knew him not.   *1 John 3:1*

In this was manifested the love of God toward us, because that God sent his only begotten Son into the world, that we might live through him. Herein is love, not that we loved God, but that he loved us, and sent his Son *to be* the propitiation for our sins.   *1 John 4:9-10*

And he will love thee, and bless thee, and multiply thee.   *Deuteronomy 7:13*

For I am persuaded, that neither death, nor
life, nor angels, nor principalities, nor powers,
nor things present, nor things to come, Nor
height, nor depth, nor any other creature,
shall be able to separate us from the love of
God, which is in Christ Jesus our Lord.

Romans 8:38-39

For the Father himself loveth you, because ye
have loved me, and have believed that I came
out from God. *John 16:27*

He that loveth me shall be loved of my Father,
and I will love him, and will manifest myself
to him. *John 14:21*

But God commendeth his love toward us, in
that, while we were yet sinners, Christ died
for us. *Romans 5:8*

That Christ may dwell in your hearts by faith;
that ye, being rooted and grounded in love,
May be able to comprehend with all saints
what *is* the breadth, and length, and depth,
and height; And to know the love of Christ,
which passeth knowledge, that ye might be
filled with all the fullness of God.

Ephesians 3:17-19

And we have known and believed the love that
God hath to us. God is love; and he that
dwelleth in love dwelleth in God, and God in
him...We love him, because he first loved us.

1 John 4:16, 19

New Life

Therefore if any man *be* in Christ, *he is* a
new creature: old things are passed away;
behold, all things are become new.

2 Corinthians 5:17

Who his own self bare our sins in his own
body on the tree, that we, being dead to sins,
should live unto righteousness.   *1 Peter 2:24*

Therefore we are buried with him by baptism
into death: that like as Christ was raised up
from the dead by the glory of the Father, even
so we also should walk in newness of life.

Romans 6:4

I am crucified with Christ: nevertheless I live;
yet not I, but Christ liveth in me: and the life
which I now live in the flesh I live by the faith
of the Son of God, who loved me, and gave
himself for me.   *Galatians 2:20*

Whosoever is born of God doth not commit sin; for his seed remaineth in him: and he cannot sin, because he is born of God.   *1 John 3:9*

But we all, with open face beholding as in a glass the glory of the Lord, are changed into the same image from glory to glory, *even* as by the Spirit of the Lord.   *2 Corinthians 3:18*

A new heart also will I give you, and a new spirit will I put within you: and I will take away the stony heart out of your flesh, and I will give you an heart of flesh.   *Ezekiel 36:26*

Peace

Peace I leave with you, my peace I give unto you: not as the world giveth, give I unto you. Let not your heart be troubled, neither let it be afraid.   *John 14:27*

And the peace of God, which passeth all understanding, shall keep your hearts and minds through Christ Jesus.   *Philippians 4:7*

Thou wilt keep *him* in perfect peace, *whose* mind *is* stayed *on thee:* because he trusteth in thee.   *Isaiah 26:3*

The LORD will bless his people with peace.
Psalm 29:11

He will speak peace unto his people, and to his
saints: but let them not turn again to folly.
Psalm 85:8

But the meek shall inherit the earth; and
shall delight themselves in the abundance of
peace.   *Psalm 37:11*

LORD, thou wilt ordain peace for us.
Isaiah 26:12

To be spiritually minded *is* life and peace.
Romans 8:6

But he *was* wounded for our transgressions,
he was bruised for our iniquities: the chas-
tisement of our peace *was* upon him; and with
his stripes we are healed.   *Isaiah 53:5*

For he is our peace, who hath made both one,
and hath broken down the middle wall of par-
tition *between us;* Having abolished in his
flesh the enmity, *even* the law of commandments *contained* in ordinances; for to make in
himself of twain one new man, *so* making
peace.   *Ephesians 2:15*

Therefore being justified by faith, we have peace with God through our Lord Jesus Christ. *Romans 5:1*

Great peace have they which love thy law: and nothing shall offend them. *Psalm 119:165*

When a man's ways please the LORD, he maketh even his enemies to be at peace with him. *Proverbs 16:7*

And the work of righteousness shall be peace; and the effect of righteousness quietness and assurance for ever. *Isaiah 32:17*

Prosperity

Beloved, I wish above all things that thou mayest prosper and be in health, even as thy soul prospereth. *3 John 2*

Keep therefore the words of this covenant, and do them, that ye may prosper in all that ye do. *Deuteronomy 29:9*

I, *even* I, have spoken; yea, I have called him: I have brought him, and he shall make his way prosperous. *Isaiah 48:15*

Only be thou strong and very courageous, that thou mayest observe to do according to all the law...turn not from it *to* the right hand or *to* the left, that thou mayest prosper whithersoever thou goest. This book of the law shall not depart out of thy mouth; but thou shalt meditate therein day and night, that thou mayest observe to do according to all that is written therein: for then thou shalt make thy way prosperous, and then thou shalt have good success. *Joshua 1:7-8*

Pray for the peace of Jerusalem: they shall prosper that love thee. Peace be within thy walls, *and* prosperity within thy palaces.
Psalm 122:6-7

Believe in the Lord your God, so shall ye be established; believe his prophets, so shall ye prosper. *2 Chronicles 20:20*

Blessed is the man that walketh not in the counsel of the ungodly...But his delight is the law of the Lord; and in his law doth he meditate day and night. And he shall be like a tree planted by the rivers of water, that bringeth forth his fruit in his season; his leaf also shall not wither; and whatsoever he doeth shall prosper. *Psalm 1:1-3*

Let the LORD be magnified, which hath pleasure in the prosperity of his servant.   *Psalm 35:27*

For the seed *shall be* prosperous; the vine shall give her fruit, and the ground shall give her increase, and the heavens shall give their dew; and I will cause the remnant of this people to possess all these *things*. And it shall come to pass, *that* as ye were a curse among the heathen, O house of Judah, and house of Israel; so will I save you, and ye shall be a blessing: fear not, *but* let your hands be strong.   *Zechariah 8:12-13*

Behold, I will bring it health and cure, and I will cure them, and will reveal unto them the abundance of peace and truth...And it shall be to me a name of joy, a praise and an honor before all the nations of the earth, which shall hear all the good that I do unto them: and they shall fear and tremble for all the goodness and for all the prosperity that I procure unto it.   *Jeremiah 33:6, 9*

But thou shalt remember the LORD thy God: for *it is* he that giveth thee power to get wealth, that he may establish his covenant which he sware unto thy fathers, as *it is* this day.   *Deuteronomy 8:18*

If they obey and serve *him,* they shall spend their days in prosperity, and their years in pleasures.   *Job 36:11*

Protection

For the LORD God *is* a sun and shield: the LORD will give grace and glory: no good *thing* will he withhold from them that walk uprightly.   *Psalm 84:11*

He will keep the feet of his saints, and the wicked shall be silent in darkness; for by strength shall no man prevail.   *1 Samuel 2:9*

For thou, LORD, wilt bless the righteous; with favor wilt thou compass him as *with* a shield.
                                        Psalm 5:12

O love the LORD, all ye his saints: *for* the LORD preserveth the faithful.   *Psalm 31:23*

They that trust in the LORD *shall be* as mount Zion, *which* cannot be removed, *but* abideth for ever. As the mountains *are* round about Jerusalem, so the LORD *is* round about his people from henceforth even for ever.
                                        Psalm 125:1-2

For he shall give his angels charge over thee, to keep thee in all thy ways. They shall bear thee up in *their* hands, lest thou dash thy foot against a stone. *Psalm 91:11-12*

Surely he shall deliver thee from the snare of the fowler, *and* from the noisome pestilence. He shall cover thee with his feathers, and under his wings shalt thou trust: his truth *shall be thy* shield and buckler. *Psalm 91:3-4*

For who *is* God save the LORD? or who *is* a rock save our God? *It is* God that girdeth me with strength, and maketh my way perfect. *Psalm 18:31-32*

The LORD *is* my rock, and my fortress, and my deliverer; my God, my strength, in whom I will trust; my buckler, and the horn of my salvation, *and* my high tower. *Psalm 18:2*

The LORD *is* thy keeper: the LORD *is* thy shade upon thy right hand. The sun shall not smite thee by day, nor the moon by night. The LORD shall preserve thee from all evil: he shall preserve thy soul. The LORD shall preserve thy going out and thy coming in from this time forth, and even for evermore. *Psalm 121:5-8*

Every word of God *is* pure: he *is* a shield unto them that put their trust in him.

Proverbs 30:5

Many *are* the afflictions of the righteous: but the LORD delivereth him out of them all.

Psalm 34:19

Righteousness

For with the heart man believeth unto righteousness; and with the mouth confession is made unto salvation. *Romans 10:10*

But of him [God] are ye in Christ Jesus, who of God is made unto us wisdom, and righteousness, and sanctification, and redemption.

1 Corinthians 1:30

For he hath made him *to be* sin for us, who knew no sin; that we might be made the righteousness of God in him. *2 Corinthians 5:21*

For if by one man's offense death reigned by one; much more they which receive abundance of grace and of the gift of righteousness shall reign in life by one, Jesus Christ.

Romans 5:17

For the fruit of the Spirit is in all goodness and righteousness and truth. *Ephesians 5:9*

Now the righteousness of God without the law is manifested...Even the righteousness of God *which is* by faith of Jesus Christ unto all and upon all them that believe. *Romans 3:21-22*

And be found in him, not having mine own righteousness, which is of the law, but that which is through the faith of Christ, the righteousness which is of God by faith.
Philippians 3:9

Now to him that worketh is the reward not reckoned of grace, but of debt. But to him that worketh not, but believeth on him that justifieth the ungodly, his faith is counted for righteousness. *Romans 4:4-5*

And if Christ *be* in you...the Spirit *is* life because of righteousness. *Romans 8:10*

Safety

I will both lay me down in peace, and sleep: for thou, LORD, only makest me dwell in safety. Psalm 4:8

Wherefore ye shall do my statutes, and keep my judgments, and do them; and ye shall dwell in the land in safety.   *Leviticus 25:18*

The God of my rock; in him will I trust: *he is* my shield, and the horn of my salvation, my high tower, and my refuge, my savior; thou savest me from violence.   *2 Samuel 22:3*

The beloved of the LORD shall dwell in safety by him; *and the LORD* shall cover him all the day long, and he shall dwell between his shoulders.   *Deuteronomy 33:12*

Though I walk in the midst of trouble, thou wilt revive me: thou shalt stretch forth thine hand against the wrath of mine enemies, and thy right hand shall save me.   *Psalm 138:7*

For the oppression of the poor, for the sighing of the needy, now will I arise, saith the LORD; I will set *him* in safety *from him that* puffeth at him.   *Psalm 12:5*

He that dwelleth in the secret place of the most High shall abide under the shadow of the Almighty. I will say of the LORD, *He is* my refuge and my fortress: my God; in him will I trust.   Psalm 91:1-2

If thou prepare thine heart, and stretch out thine hands toward him...thou shalt be secure, because there is hope; yea, thou shalt dig *about thee, and* thou shalt take thy rest in safety. *Job 11:13, 18*

Where no counsel *is,* the people fall: but in the multitude of counselors *there is* safety.

Proverbs 11:14

The fear of man bringeth a snare: but whoso putteth his trust in the LORD shall be safe.

Proverbs 29:25

The name of the LORD *is* a strong tower: the righteous runneth into it, and is safe.

Proverbs 18:10

Salvation

For God sent not his Son into the world to condemn the world; but that the world through him might be saved. *John 3:17*

For this *is* good and acceptable in the sight of God our Savior; Who will have all men to be saved, and to come unto the knowledge of the truth. *1 Timothy 2:3-4*

If thou shalt confess with thy mouth the Lord
Jesus, and shalt believe in thine heart that God
hath raised him from the dead, thou shalt be
saved. For with the heart man believeth unto
righteousness; and with the mouth confession
is made unto salvation.   *Romans 10:9-10*

And she shall bring forth a son, and thou shalt
call his name JESUS: for he shall save his people
from their sins.   *Matthew 1:21*

For whosoever shall call upon the name of the
Lord shall be saved.   *Romans 10:13*

For if, when we were enemies, we were reconciled to God by the death of his Son, much
more, being reconciled, we shall be saved by
his life.   *Romans 5:10*

With long life will I satisfy him, and show him
my salvation.   *Psalm 91:16*

For the LORD taketh pleasure in his people: he
will beautify the meek with salvation.
                                    Psalm 149:4

For God hath not appointed us to wrath, but
to obtain salvation by our Lord Jesus Christ.
                              1 Thessalonians 5:9

For by grace are ye saved through faith; and that not of yourselves: *it is* the gift of God: Not of works, lest any man should boast.
Ephesians 2:8-9

In whom ye also *trusted,* after that ye heard the word of truth, the gospel of your salvation: in whom also after that ye believed, ye were sealed with that holy Spirit of promise.
Ephesians 1:13

I am the door: by me if any man enter in, he shall be saved, and shall go in and out, and find pasture.
John 10:9

And they said, Believe on the Lord Jesus Christ, and thou shalt be saved, and thy house.
Acts 16:31

Not by works of righteousness which we have done, but according to his mercy he saved us, by the washing of regeneration, and renewing of the Holy Ghost; Which he shed on us abundantly through Jesus Christ our Savior; That being justified by his grace, we should be made heirs according to the hope of eternal life.
Titus 3:5-7

Satisfaction

With long life will I satisfy him, and show him my salvation.   *Psalm 91:16*

Behold, I will send you corn, and wine, and oil, and ye shall be satisfied therewith...And ye shall eat in plenty, and be satisfied, and praise the name of the LORD your God, that hath dealt wondrously with you: and my people shall never be ashamed.   *Joel 2:19, 26*

And I will satiate the soul of the priests with fatness, and my people shall be satisfied with my goodness, saith the LORD.   *Jeremiah 31:14*

The fear of the LORD *tendeth* to life: and *he that hath it* shall abide satisfied; he shall not be visited with evil.   Proverbs 19:23

The LORD shall guide thee continually, and satisfy thy soul in drought, and make fat thy bones: and thou shalt be like a watered garden, and like a spring of water, whose waters fail not.   *Isaiah 58:11*

The meek shall eat and be satisfied: they shall praise the LORD that seek him: your heart shall live for ever.   *Psalm 22:26*

Oh that *men* would praise the LORD *for* his goodness, and *for* his wonderful works to the children of men! For he satisfieth the longing soul, and filleth the hungry soul with goodness.
Psalm 107:8-9

A man shall be satisfied with good by the fruit of *his* mouth: and the recompense of a man's hands shall be rendered unto him.
Proverbs 12:14

Ho, every one that thirsteth, come ye to the waters, and he that hath no money; come ye, buy, and eat; yea, come, buy wine and milk without money and without price. Wherefore do ye spend money for *that which is* not bread? and your labor for *that which* satisfieth not? hearken diligently unto me, and eat ye *that which is* good, and let your soul delight itself in fatness. Incline your ear, and come unto me: hear, and your soul shall live; and I will make an everlasting covenant with you, *even* the sure mercies of David.
Isaiah 55:1-3

And Jesus said unto them, I am the bread of life: he that cometh to me shall never hunger; and he that believeth on me shall never thirst.
John 6:35

Be content with such things as ye have: for he hath said, I will never leave thee, nor forsake thee.   *Hebrews 13:5*

Who satisfieth thy mouth with good *things; so that* thy youth is renewed like the eagle's.

Psalm 103:5

How excellent *is* thy lovingkindness, O God! therefore the children of men put their trust under the shadow of thy wings. They shall be abundantly satisfied with the fatness of thy house; and thou shalt make them drink of the river of thy pleasures.   *Psalm 36:7-8*

Spiritual Gifts

For the gifts and calling of God *are* without repentance.   *Romans 11:29*

If ye then, being evil, know how to give good gifts unto your children: how much more shall *your* heavenly Father give the Holy Spirit to them that ask him?   *Luke 11:13*

So that ye come behind in no gift; waiting for the coming of our Lord Jesus Christ.

1 Corinthians 1:7

Now concerning spiritual *gifts*....there are diversities of gifts, but the same Spirit. And there are differences of administrations, but the same Lord. And there are diversities of operations, but it is the same God which worketh all in all. But the manifestation of the Spirit is given to every man to profit withal. For to one is given by the Spirit the word of wisdom; to another the word of knowledge by the same Spirit; To another faith by the same Spirit; to another the gifts of healing by the same Spirit; To another the working of miracles; to another prophecy; to another discerning of spirits; to another *divers* kinds of tongues; to another the interpretation of tongues: But all these worketh that one and the selfsame Spirit, dividing to every man severally as he will.   *1 Corinthians 12:1, 4-11*

Even so ye, forasmuch as ye are zealous of spiritual *gifts,* seek that ye may excel to the edifying of the church.   *1 Corinthians 14:12*

So we, *being* many, are one body in Christ, and every one members one of another. Having then gifts differing according to the grace that is given to us, whether prophecy...ministry... teaching...exhortation, or he that giveth... ruleth...[or] showeth mercy.   *Romans 12:5-8*

I have filled him with the spirit of God, in wisdom, and in understanding, and in knowledge, and in all manner of workmanship, To devise cunning works, to work in gold, and in silver, and in brass, And in cutting of stones, to set *them*, and in carving of timber, to work in all manner of workmanship.   *Exodus 31:3-5*

Wherefore he saith, When he ascended up on high, he led captivity captive, and gave gifts unto men.   *Ephesians 4:8*

Spiritual Maturity

The righteous shall flourish like the palm tree: he shall grow like a cedar in Lebanon. Those that be planted in the house of the LORD shall flourish in the courts of our God.
                                    Psalm 92:12-13

That we *henceforth* be no more children, tossed to and fro, and carried about with every wind of doctrine...But speaking the truth in love, may grow up into him in all things, which is the head, *even* Christ.   *Ephesians 4:14-15*

And ye shall go forth, and grow up.
                                    Malachi 4:2

And he shall be like a tree planted by the rivers of water, that bringeth forth his fruit in his season; his leaf also shall not wither; and whatsoever he doeth shall prosper. *Psalm 1:3*

Beside this, giving all diligence, add to your faith virtue; and to virtue knowledge...For if these things be in you, and abound, they make *you that ye shall* neither *be* barren nor unfruitful in the knowledge of our Lord Jesus Christ. *2 Peter 1:5, 8*

Now therefore ye are ...fellowcitizens with the saints, and of the household of God; And are built upon the foundation of the apostles and prophets, Jesus Christ himself being the chief corner *stone;* In whom all the building fitly framed together groweth unto an holy temple in the Lord: In whom ye also are builded together for an habitation of God through the Spirit. *Ephesians 2:19-22*

But the path of the just *is* as the shining light, that shineth more and more unto the perfect day. *Proverbs 4:18*

And to know the love of Christ, which passeth knowledge, that ye might be filled with all the fullness of God. *Ephesians 3:19*

But we all, with open face beholding as in a glass the glory of the Lord, are changed into the same image from glory to glory, *even* as by the Spirit of the Lord.   *2 Corinthians 3:18*

Being confident of this very thing, that he which hath begun a good work in you will perform *it* until the day of Jesus Christ.
                                    Philippians 1:6

That ye might walk worthy of the Lord unto all pleasing, being fruitful in every good work, and increasing in the knowledge of God.
                                    Colossians 1:10

As newborn babes, desire the sincere milk of the word, that ye may grow thereby: If so be ye have tasted that the Lord *is* gracious.
                                    1 Peter 2:2-3

Therefore leaving the principles of the doctrine of Christ, let us go on unto perfection.
                                    Hebrews 6:1

According as his divine power hath given unto us all things that *pertain* unto life and godliness, through the knowledge of him that hath called us to glory and virtue.   *2 Peter 1:3*

And this I pray, that your love may abound yet more and more in knowledge and *in* all judgment; That ye may approve things that are excellent; that ye may be sincere and without offense till the day of Christ; Being filled with the fruits of righteousness, which are by Jesus Christ, unto the glory and praise of God.   *Philippians 1:9-11*

But grow in grace, and *in* the knowledge of our Lord and Savior Jesus Christ. To him *be* glory both now and for ever.   *2 Peter 3:18*

Strength

He giveth power to the faint; and to *them that have* no might he increaseth strength.
     Isaiah 40:29

Glory and honor *are* in his presence; strength and gladness *are* in his place.
     1 Chronicles 16:27

The LORD will give strength unto his people.
     Psalm 29:11

Trust ye in the LORD for ever: for in the LORD JEHOVAH *is* everlasting strength.   *Isaiah 26:4*

Both riches and honor *come* of thee, and thou reignest over all; and in thine hand *is* power and might; and in thine hand *it is* to make great, and to give strength unto all.

1 Chronicles 29:12

The LORD *is* my strength and my shield; my heart trusted in him, and I am helped: therefore my heart greatly rejoiceth; and with my song will I praise him.   *Psalm 28:7*

The LORD *is* my light and my salvation; whom shall I fear? the LORD *is* the strength of my life; of whom shall I be afraid?   *Psalm 27:1*

Blessed *is* the man whose strength *is* in thee; in whose heart *are* the ways *of them*...They go from strength to strength, *every one of them* in Zion appeareth before God.   *Psalm 84:5, 7*

It is God that girdeth me with strength, and maketh my way perfect.   *Psalm 18:32*

The joy of the LORD is your strength.

Nehemiah 8:10

But the salvation of the righteous *is* of the LORD: *he is* their strength in the time of trouble.   *Psalm 37:39*

They that wait upon the LORD shall renew *their* strength; they shall mount up with wings as eagles; they shall run, and not be weary; *and* they shall walk, and not faint.

Isaiah 40:31

A wise man *is* strong; yea, a man of knowledge increaseth strength.   *Proverbs 24:5*

Be strong in the Lord, and in the power of his might.   *Ephesians 6:10*

Thy God hath commanded thy strength: strengthen, O God, that which thou hast wrought for us.   *Psalm 68:28*

In the day when I cried thou answeredst me, *and* strengthenedst me *with* strength in my soul.   *Psalm 138:3*

My flesh and my heart faileth: *but* God *is* the strength of my heart, and my portion for ever.

Psalm 73:26

And he said unto me, My grace is sufficient for thee: for my strength is made perfect in weakness. Most gladly therefore will I rather glory in my infirmities, that the power of Christ may rest upon me.   *2 Corinthians 12:9*

The way of the LORD *is* strength to the upright. *Proverbs 10:29*

We also...do not cease to pray for you...that ye might be filled with the knowledge of his will in all wisdom and spiritual understanding; That ye might walk worthy of the Lord unto all pleasing, being fruitful in every good work, and increasing in the knowledge of God; Strengthened with all might, according to his glorious power, unto all patience and longsuffering with joyfulness. *Colossians 1:9-11*

I will strengthen thee; yea, I will help thee; yea, I will uphold thee with the right hand of my righteousness. *Isaiah 41:10*

I can do all things through Christ which strengtheneth me. *Philippians 4:13*

Success

This book of the law shall not depart out of thy mouth; but thou shalt meditate therein day and night, that thou mayest observe to do according to all that is written therein: for then thou shalt make thy way prosperous, and then thou shalt have good success. *Joshua 1:8*

Thou shalt keep therefore his statutes, and his commandments, which I command thee this day, that it may go well with thee, and with thy children after thee, and that thou mayest prolong *thy* days upon the earth, which the LORD thy God giveth thee, for ever.

Deuteronomy 4:40

Hear therefore, O Israel, and observe to do *it;* that it may be well with thee, and that ye may increase mightily, as the LORD God of thy fathers hath promised thee, in the land that floweth with milk and honey. *Deuteronomy 6:3*

The LORD, before whom I walk, will send his angel with thee, and prosper thy way.

Genesis 24:40

I [wisdom] love them that love me; and those that seek me early shall find me. Riches and honor *are* with me; *yea,* durable riches and righteousness. My fruit *is* better than gold, yea, than fine gold; and my revenue than choice silver. I lead in the way of righteousness, in the midst of the paths of judgment: That I may cause those that love me to inherit substance; and I will fill their treasures.

Proverbs 8:17-21

The LORD *was* with him, and...made all that he did to prosper in his hand.   *Genesis 39:3*

As long as he sought the LORD, God made him to prosper.   *2 Chronicles 26:5*

Thou hast dealt well with thy servant, O LORD, according unto thy word. *Psalm 119:65*

Then shalt thou prosper, if thou takest heed to fulfill the statutes and judgments which the LORD charged Moses with concerning Israel: be strong, and of good courage; dread not, nor be dismayed.   *1 Chronicles 22:13*

Truth

[God] Who will have all men to be saved, and to come unto the knowledge of the truth.
                                      1 Timothy 2:4

Then said Jesus...If ye continue in my word, *then* are ye my disciples indeed; And ye shall know the truth, and the truth shall make you free.   *John 8:31-32*

For the fruit of the Spirit is in all goodness and righteousness and truth.   *Ephesians 5:9*

For the truth's sake, which dwelleth in us, and shall be with us for ever. Grace be with you, mercy, *and* peace, from God the Father, and from the Lord Jesus Christ, the Son of the Father, in truth and love.   *2 John 2-3*

But when the Comforter is come, whom I will send unto you from the Father, *even* the Spirit of truth, which proceedeth from the Father, he shall testify of me.   *John 15:26*

Howbeit when he, the Spirit of truth, is come, he will guide you into all truth: for he shall not speak of himself; but whatsoever he shall hear, *that* shall he speak: and he will show you things to come.   *John 16:13*

But thou, O Lord, *art* a God full of compassion, and gracious, longsuffering, and plenteous in mercy and truth.   *Psalm 86:15*

All the paths of the LORD *are* mercy and truth unto such as keep his covenant and his testimonies.   *Psalm 25:10*

Behold, thou desirest truth in the inward parts: and in the hidden *part* thou shalt make me to know wisdom.   *Psalm 51:6*

Wisdom

For wisdom *is* better than rubies; and all the things that may be desired are not to be compared to it. I wisdom dwell with prudence, and find out knowledge of witty inventions.

Proverbs 8:11-12

For *God* giveth to a man that *is* good in his sight wisdom, and knowledge.

Ecclesiastes 2:26

For the LORD giveth wisdom: out of his mouth *cometh* knowledge and understanding. He layeth up sound wisdom for the righteous: *he is* a buckler to them that walk uprightly.

Proverbs 2:6-7

The fear of the LORD *is* the beginning of wisdom: and the knowledge of the holy *is* understanding.　　　　　　　　　*Proverbs 9:10*

With him *is* wisdom and strength, he hath counsel and understanding.　　　*Job 12:13*

If any of you lack wisdom, let him ask of God, that giveth to all *men* liberally, and upbraideth not; and it shall be given him.

James 1:5

Blessed be the name of God for ever and ever: for wisdom and might are his...he giveth wisdom unto the wise, and knowledge to them that know understanding: He revealeth the deep and secret things.   *Daniel 2:20-22*

When wisdom entereth into thine heart, and knowledge is pleasant unto thy soul.
Proverbs 2:10

But of him are ye in Christ Jesus, who of God is made unto us wisdom.   *1 Corinthians 1:30*

Wisdom and knowledge *is* granted unto thee.
2 Chronicles 1:12

Behold, thou desirest truth in the inward parts: and in the hidden *part* thou shalt make me to know wisdom.   *Psalm 51:6*

Your Heart's Desires

Delight thyself also in the LORD; and he shall give thee the desires of thine heart.
Psalm 37:4

The desire of the righteous shall be granted.
Proverbs 10:24

Thou openest thine hand, and satisfiest the desire of every living thing.   *Psalm 145:16*

But now they desire a better *country,* that is, an heavenly: wherefore God is not ashamed to be called their God: for he hath prepared for them a city.   *Hebrews 11:16*

Thou hast given him his heart's desire, and hast not withholden the request of his lips.
                                              Psalm 21:2

Who satisfieth thy mouth with good *things; so that* thy youth is renewed like the eagle's.
                                             Psalm 103:5

I thank thee, and praise thee, O thou God of my fathers, who hast given me wisdom and might, and hast made known unto me now what we desired of thee.   *Daniel 2:23*

LORD, thou hast heard the desire of the humble: thou wilt prepare their heart, thou wilt cause thine ear to hear: To judge the fatherless and the oppressed, that the man of the earth may no more oppress.   *Psalm 10:18*

The God of my mercy shall prevent me: God shall let me see *my desire*.   *Psalm 59:10*

Whom have I in heaven *but thee?* and *there is* none upon earth *that* I desire beside thee. My flesh and my heart faileth: *but* God *is* the strength of my heart, and my portion for ever.
Psalm 73:25-26

What things soever ye desire, when ye pray, believe that ye receive *them*, and ye shall have *them*. *Mark 11:24*

He will fulfill the desire of them that fear him.
Psalm 145:19

He bringeth them unto their desired haven.
Psalm 107:30

A good man showeth favor, and lendeth: he will guide his affairs with discretion...His heart *is* established, he shall not be afraid, until he see *his desire*. *Psalm 112:5, 8*

Bible Promises for Those Who Are...

Afraid

What time I am afraid, I will trust in thee. In God I will praise his word, in God I have put my trust; I will not fear what flesh can do unto me. *Psalm 56:3-4*

For I the LORD thy God will hold thy right hand, saying unto thee, Fear not; I will help thee. *Isaiah 41:13*

The LORD *is* my light and my salvation; whom shall I fear? the LORD *is* the strength of my life; of whom shall I be afraid? *Psalm 27:1*

113

He shall cover thee with his feathers, and under his wings shalt thou trust: his truth *shall be thy* shield and buckler. Thou shalt not be afraid for the terror by night; *nor* for the arrow *that* flieth by day; *Nor* for the pestilence *that* walketh in darkness; *nor* for the destruction *that* wasteth at noonday.   *Psalm 91:4-6*

Blessed *is* the man *that* feareth the LORD, *that* delighteth greatly in his commandments...He shall not be afraid of evil tidings: his heart is fixed, trusting in the LORD. His heart *is* established, he shall not be afraid. *Psalm 112:1, 7-8*

Fear thou not; for I *am* with thee: be not dismayed; for I *am* thy God: I will strengthen thee; yea, I will help thee; yea, I will uphold thee with the right hand of my righteousness.
Isaiah 41:10

Say to them *that are* of a fearful heart, Be strong, fear not: behold, your God will come *with* vengeance, *even* God *with* a recompense; he will come and save you.   *Isaiah 35:4*

But now thus saith the LORD that created thee...Fear not: for I have redeemed thee, I have called *thee* by thy name; thou *art* mine.
Isaiah 43:1

There is no fear in love; but perfect love casteth out fear.   *1 John 4:18*

When thou goest out to battle against thine enemies, and seest horses, and chariots, *and* a people more than thou, be not afraid of them: for the LORD thy God *is* with thee, which brought thee up out of the land of Egypt... Hear, O Israel, ye approach this day unto battle against your enemies: let not your hearts faint, fear not, and do not tremble, neither be ye terrified because of them; For the LORD your God *is* he that goeth with you, to fight for you against your enemies, to save you.   *Deuteronomy 20:1, 3-4*

Fear not, little flock; for it is your Father's good pleasure to give you the kingdom.
                    Luke 12:32

Be not afraid of sudden fear, neither of the desolation of the wicked, when it cometh. For the LORD shall be thy confidence, and shall keep thy foot from being taken.
                    Proverbs 3:25-26

God hath not given us the spirit of fear; but of power, and of love, and of a sound mind.
                    2 Timothy 1:7

Fear not: for they that *be* with us *are* more
than they that *be* with them.　　*2 Kings 6:16*

Be strong and of good courage, and do *it:* fear
not, nor be dismayed: for the LORD God, *even*
my God, *will be* with thee; he will not fail
thee, nor forsake thee.　　*1 Chronicles 28:20*

Are not five sparrows sold for two farthings,
and not one of them is forgotten before God?
But even the very hairs of your head are all
numbered. Fear not therefore: ye are of more
value than many sparrows.　　*Luke 12:6-7*

Backslidden

For thus saith the high and lofty One that in-
habiteth eternity, whose name *is* Holy; I dwell
in the high and holy *place,* with him also *that
is* of a contrite and humble spirit, to revive the
spirit of the humble, and to revive the heart of
the contrite ones...I have seen his ways, and
will heal him: I will lead him also, and restore
comforts unto him and to his mourners. I cre-
ate the fruit of the lips; Peace, peace to *him
that is* far off, and to *him that is* near, saith
the LORD; and I will heal him.

　　　　　　　　　　　　　Isaiah 57:15, 18-19

Return, thou backsliding Israel, saith the LORD; *and* I will not cause mine anger to fall upon you: for I *am* merciful, saith the LORD, *and* I will not keep *anger* for ever. Only acknowledge thine iniquity, that thou hast transgressed against the LORD thy God, and hast scattered thy ways to the strangers under every green tree, and ye have not obeyed my voice, saith the LORD. Turn, O backsliding children, saith the LORD; for I am married unto you: and I will take you one of a city, and two of a family, and I will bring you to Zion.

Jeremiah 3:12-14

O Israel, return unto the LORD thy God; for thou hast fallen by thine iniquity. Take with you words, and turn to the LORD: say unto him, Take away all iniquity, and receive *us* graciously: so will we render the calves of our lips. Asshur shall not save us; we will not ride upon horses: neither will we say any more to the work of our hands, *Ye are* our gods: for in thee the fatherless findeth mercy. I will heal their backsliding, I will love them freely: for mine anger is turned away from him.   *Hosea 14:1-4*

I have blotted out, as a thick cloud, thy transgressions, and, as a cloud, thy sins: return unto me; for I have redeemed thee.   *Isaiah 44:22*

A voice was heard upon the high places, weeping *and* supplications of the children of Israel: for they have perverted their way, *and* they have forgotten the LORD their God. Return, ye backsliding children, *and* I will heal your backslidings. Behold, we come unto thee; for thou *art* the LORD our God.

Jeremiah 3:21-22

All we like sheep have gone astray; we have turned every one to his own way; and the LORD hath laid on him the iniquity of us all.

Isaiah 53:6

Come now, and let us reason together, saith the LORD: though your sins be as scarlet, they shall be as white as snow; though they be red like crimson, they shall be as wool.

Isaiah 1:18

For I will set mine eyes upon them for good, and I will bring them again to this land: and I will build them, and not pull *them* down; and I will plant them, and not pluck *them* up. And I will give them an heart to know me, that I *am* the LORD: and they shall be my people, and I will be their God: for they shall return unto me with their whole heart.

Jeremiah 24:6-7

Brokenhearted

The LORD *is* nigh unto them that are of a broken heart; and saveth such as be of a contrite spirit. *Psalm 34:18*

Thou tellest my wanderings: put thou my tears into thy bottle: *are they* not in thy book? When I cry *unto thee,* then shall mine enemies turn back: this I know; for God *is* for me.
Psalm 56:8-9

He healeth the broken in heart, and bindeth up their wounds. *Psalm 147:3*

He hath sent me to heal the brokenhearted, ...to set at liberty them that are bruised.
Luke 4:18

Sing, O heavens; and be joyful, O earth; and break forth into singing, O mountains: for the LORD hath comforted his people, and will have mercy upon his afflicted. *Isaiah 49:13*

The spirit of the Lord GOD *is* upon me; because the LORD hath anointed me to preach good tidings unto the meek; he hath sent me to bind up the brokenhearted...to comfort all that mourn. *Isaiah 61:1-2*

The sacrifices of God *are* a broken spirit: a broken and a contrite heart, O God, thou wilt not despise.   *Psalm 51:17*

Weeping may endure for a night, but joy *cometh* in the morning.   *Psalm 30:5*

Burdened

Is not this the fast that I have chosen? to loose the bands of wickedness, to undo the heavy burdens, and to let the oppressed go free, and that ye break every yoke?   *Isaiah 58:6*

And it shall come to pass in that day, *that* his burden shall be taken away from off thy shoulder, and his yoke from off thy neck, and the yoke shall be destroyed because of the anointing.   *Isaiah 10:27*

Thou wilt surely wear away, both thou, and this people that *is* with thee: for this thing *is* too heavy for thee; thou art not able to perform it thyself alone...And it shall be, *that* every great matter they shall bring unto thee, but every small matter they shall judge: so shall it be easier for thyself, and they shall bear *the burden* with thee.   *Exodus 18:18, 22*

[The LORD] which keepeth truth for ever... raiseth them that are bowed down: the LORD loveth the righteous.   *Psalm 146:6, 8*

Come unto me, all *ye* that labor and are heavy laden, and I will give you rest. Take my yoke upon you, and learn of me; for I am meek and lowly in heart: and ye shall find rest unto your souls. For my yoke *is* easy, and my burden is light.   *Matthew 11:28-30*

Blessed *be* the Lord, *who* daily loadeth us *with benefits, even* the God of our salvation.
            Psalm 68:19

I removed his shoulder from the burden: his hands were delivered from the pots. Thou calledst in trouble, and I delivered thee; I answered thee in the secret place of thunder.
            Psalm 81:6-7

For thou hast broken the yoke of his burden, and the staff of his shoulder, the rod of his oppressor...For unto us a child is born, unto us a son is given: and the government shall be upon his shoulder: and his name shall be called Wonderful, Counselor, The mighty God, The everlasting Father, The Prince of Peace.
            Isaiah 9:4, 6

Cast thy burden upon the LORD, and he shall sustain thee: he shall never suffer the righteous to be moved . *Psalm 55:22*

Casting all your care upon him; for he careth for you. *1 Peter 5:7*

Confused

And thine ears shall hear a word behind thee, saying, This *is* the way, walk ye in it, when ye turn to the right hand, and when ye turn to the left. *Isaiah 30:21*

If any of you lack wisdom, let him ask of God, that giveth to all *men* liberally, and upbraideth not; and it shall be given him. But let him ask in faith, nothing wavering. For he that wavereth is like a wave of the sea driven with the wind and tossed. For let not that man think that he shall receive any thing of the Lord. A double minded man *is* unstable in all his ways. *James 1:5-8*

But he that is spiritual judgeth all things ...For who hath known the mind of the Lord, that he may instruct him? But we have the mind of Christ. *1 Corinthians 2:15-16*

And I will bring the blind by a way *that* they knew not; I will lead them in paths *that* they have not known: I will make darkness light before them, and crooked things straight. These things will I do unto them, and not forsake them.   *Isaiah 42:16*

We are troubled on every side, yet not distressed; *we are* perplexed, but not in despair... that the life also of Jesus might be made manifest in our body. For we which live are alway delivered unto death for Jesus' sake, that the life also of Jesus might be made manifest in our mortal flesh.

     2 Corinthians 4:8, 10-11

God is not the author of confusion, but of peace.   *1 Corinthians 14:33*

They cried unto thee, and were delivered: they trusted in thee, and were not confounded.

     Psalm 22:5

For where envying and strife *is,* there *is* confusion and every evil work. But the wisdom that is from above is first pure, then peaceable, gentle, *and* easy to be entreated, full of mercy and good fruits, without partiality, and without hypocrisy.   *James 3:16-17*

For my thoughts *are* not your thoughts, neither *are* your ways my ways, saith the LORD. For *as* the heavens are higher than the earth, so are my ways higher than your ways, and my thoughts than your thoughts.   *Isaiah 55:8-9*

Thou wilt keep *him* in perfect peace, *whose* mind *is* stayed *on thee*.   *Isaiah 26:3*

Depressed

My soul melteth for heaviness: strengthen thou me according unto thy word.
                           Psalm 119:28

He brought me up also out of an horrible pit, out of the miry clay, and set my feet upon a rock, *and* established my goings.   *Psalm 40:2*

My flesh and my heart faileth: *but* God *is* the strength of my heart, and my portion for ever.
                            Psalm 73:26

The LORD also will be a refuge for the oppressed, a refuge in times of trouble. They that know thy name will put their trust in thee: for thou, LORD, hast not forsaken them that seek thee.   *Psalm 9:9-10*

Why art thou cast down, O my soul? and why art thou disquieted within me? hope in God: for I shall yet praise him, *who is* the health of my countenance, and my God.   *Psalm 43:5*

Be of good courage, and he shall strengthen your heart, all ye that hope in the LORD.
Psalm 31:24

Heaviness in the heart of man maketh it stoop: but a good word maketh it glad.
Proverbs 12:25

To appoint unto them that mourn in Zion, to give unto them beauty for ashes, the oil of joy for mourning, the garment of praise for the spirit of heaviness; that they might be called trees of righteousness, the planting of the LORD, that he might be glorified.   *Isaiah 61:3*

Neither be ye sorry; for the joy of the LORD is your strength....Hold your peace, for the day *is* holy; neither be ye grieved.   *Nehemiah 8:10-11*

Then shall the virgin rejoice in the dance, both young men and old together: for I will turn their mourning into joy, and will comfort them, and make them rejoice from their sorrow.   *Jeremiah 31:13*

Wherein ye greatly rejoice, though now for a season, if need be, ye are in heaviness through manifold temptations...Whom having not seen, ye love; in whom, though now ye see *him* not, yet believing, ye rejoice with joy unspeakable and full of glory.   *1 Peter 1:6, 8*

Thou hast turned for me my mourning into dancing: thou hast put off my sackcloth, and girded me with gladness.   *Psalm 30:11*

And the ransomed of the LORD shall return, and come to Zion with songs and everlasting joy upon their heads: they shall obtain joy and gladness, and sorrow and sighing shall flee away.   *Isaiah 35:10*

Discouraged

A bruised reed shall he not break, and the smoking flax shall he not quench: he shall bring forth judgment unto truth. He shall not fail nor be discouraged, till he have set judgment in the earth: and the isles shall wait for his law.   *Isaiah 42:3-4*

Let us not be weary in well doing: for in due season we shall reap, if we faint not.
                                      Galatians 6:9

Cast not away therefore your confidence, which hath great recompense of reward. For ye have need of patience, that, after ye have done the will of God, ye might receive the promise.   Hebrews 10:35-36

Being confident of this very thing, that he which hath begun a good work in you will perform *it* until the day of Jesus Christ.
Philippians 1:6

For thus saith the Lord GOD, the Holy One of Israel; In returning and rest shall ye be saved; in quietness and in confidence shall be your strength.   *Isaiah 30:15*

Hope maketh not ashamed; because the love of God is shed abroad in our hearts by the Holy Ghost which is given unto us.   *Romans 5:5*

We know that all things work together for good to them that love God, to them who are the called according to *his* purpose.
Romans 8:28

But verily God hath heard *me;* he hath attended to the voice of my prayer. Blessed *be* God, which hath not turned away my prayer, nor his mercy from me.   *Psalm 66:19-20*

Our soul waiteth for the LORD: he *is* our help
and our shield. For our heart shall rejoice in
him, because we have trusted in his holy
name. Let thy mercy, O LORD, be upon us, according as we hope in thee.　　　*Psalm 33:20-22*

Trust in him at all times; *ye* people, pour out
your heart before him: God *is* a refuge for us.
　　　　　　　　　　　　　　　　　　　　　Psalm 62:8

I had fainted, unless I had believed to see the
goodness of the LORD in the land of the living.
Wait on the LORD: be of good courage, and he
shall strengthen thine heart: wait, I say, on
the LORD.　　　　　　　　　　　　　*Psalm 27:13-14*

Doubting

Jesus answering saith unto them, Have faith in
God. For verily I say unto you, That whosoever
shall say unto this mountain, Be thou removed,
and be thou cast into the sea; and shall not
doubt in his heart, but shall believe that those
things which he saith shall come to pass; he
shall have whatsoever he saith. Therefore I say
unto you, What things soever ye desire, when
ye pray, believe that ye receive *them,* and ye
shall have *them.*　　　　　　　　　　*Mark 11:22-24*

Now faith is the substance of things hoped for, the evidence of things not seen...But without faith *it is* impossible to please *him:* for he that cometh to God must believe that he is, and *that* he is a rewarder of them that diligently seek him.   *Hebrews 11:1, 6*

Hast thou faith? have *it* to thyself before God. Happy *is* he that condemneth not himself in that thing which he alloweth. And he that doubteth is damned if he eat, because *he eateth* not of faith: for whatsoever *is* not of faith is sin.   *Romans 14:22-23*

Beloved, if our heart condemn us not, *then* have we confidence toward God. And whatsoever we ask, we receive of him, because we keep his commandments, and do those things that are pleasing in his sight.   *1 John 3:21-22*

If we believe not, *yet* he abideth faithful: he cannot deny himself.   *2 Timothy 2:13*

Let us draw near with a true heart in full assurance of faith, having our hearts sprinkled from an evil conscience, and our bodies washed with pure water. Let us hold fast the profession of *our* faith without wavering, for he *is* faithful that promised.   *Hebrews 10:22-23*

Jesus said unto him, If thou canst believe, all things *are* possible to him that believeth. And straightway the father of the child cried out, and said with tears, Lord, I believe; help thou mine unbelief.   *Mark 9:23-24*

I will therefore that men pray every where, lifting up holy hands, without wrath and doubting.   *1 Timothy 2:8*

Facing Death

Yea, though I walk through the valley of the shadow of death, I will fear no evil: for thou *art* with me; thy rod and thy staff they comfort me.   *Psalm 23:4*

O death, where *is* thy sting? O grave, where *is* thy victory? The sting of death *is* sin; and the strength of sin *is* the law. But thanks *be* to God, which giveth us the victory through our Lord Jesus Christ.   *1 Corinthians 15:55-57*

We are confident, *I say,* and willing rather to be absent from the body, and to be present with the Lord. Wherefore we labor, that, whether present or absent, we may be accepted of him.   *2 Corinthians 5:8-9*

For this corruptible must put on incorruption, and this mortal *must* put on immortality. So when this corruptible shall have put on incorruption, and this mortal shall have put on immortality, then shall be brought to pass the saying that is written, Death is swallowed up in victory.   *1 Corinthians 15:53-54*

In my Father's house are many mansions: if *it were* not *so,* I would have told you. I go to prepare a place for you. And if I go and prepare a place for you, I will come again, and receive you unto myself; that where I am, *there* ye may be also.   *John 14:2-3*

For I am persuaded, that neither death, nor life, nor angels, nor principalities, nor powers, nor things present, nor things to come, Nor height, nor depth, nor any other creature, shall be able to separate us from the love of God, which is in Christ Jesus our Lord.
     Romans 8:38-39

I would not have you to be ignorant, brethren, concerning them which are asleep, that ye sorrow not, even as others which have no hope. For if we believe that Jesus died and rose again, even so them also which sleep in Jesus will God bring with him.   *1 Thessalonians 4:13-14*

Jesus said unto her, I am the resurrection, and the life: he that believeth in me, though he were dead, yet shall he live.   *John 11:25*

Faithful

O love the LORD, all ye his saints: *for* the LORD preserveth the faithful.   *Psalm 31:23*

A faithful man shall abound with blessings: but he that maketh haste to be rich shall not be innocent.   *Proverbs 28:20*

He that is faithful in that which is least is faithful also in much: and he that is unjust in the least is unjust also in much.   *Luke 16:10*

Fear none of those things which thou shalt suffer: behold, the devil shall cast *some* of you into prison, that ye may be tried; and ye shall have tribulation ten days: be thou faithful unto death, and I will give thee a crown of life.
                                    Revelation 2:10

Mine eyes *shall be* upon the faithful of the land, that they may dwell with me: he that walketh in a perfect way, he shall serve me.
                                    Psalm 101:6

Let not mercy and truth forsake thee: bind them about thy neck; write them upon the table of thine heart: So shalt thou find favor and good understanding in the sight of God and man.   *Proverbs 3:3-4*

As the cold of snow in the time of harvest, *so is* a faithful messenger to them that send him: for he refresheth the soul of his masters.
Proverbs 25:13

Most men will proclaim every one his own goodness: but a faithful man who can find? The just *man* walketh in his integrity: his children *are* blessed after him.   *Proverbs 20:6-7*

Forsaken

For the LORD God, *even* my God, *will be* with thee; he will not fail thee, nor forsake thee.
1 Chronicles 28:20

Thou shalt no more be termed Forsaken; neither shall thy land any more be termed Desolate: but thou shalt be called Hephzibah, and thy land Beulah: for the LORD delighteth in thee, and thy land shall be married.
Isaiah 62:4

For the LORD thy God *is* a merciful God; he will not forsake thee, neither destroy thee, nor forget the covenant of thy fathers which he sware unto them. *Deuteronomy 4:31*

I have been young, and *now* am old; yet have I not seen the righteous forsaken...For the LORD loveth judgment, and forsaketh not his saints. *Psalm 37:25, 28*

For the LORD hath called thee as a woman forsaken and grieved in spirit, and a wife of youth, when thou wast refused, saith thy God...with great mercies will I gather thee. *Isaiah 54:6-7*

Can a woman forget her sucking child, that she should not have compassion on the son of her womb? yea, they may forget, yet will I not forget thee. *Isaiah 49:15*

They that know thy name will put their trust in thee: for thou, LORD, hast not forsaken them that seek thee. *Psalm 9:10*

For the LORD will not forsake his people for his great name's sake: because it hath pleased the LORD to make you his people. *1 Samuel 12:22*

For the LORD will not cast off his people, neither will he forsake his inheritance.

Psalm 94:14

There is a friend *that* sticketh closer than a brother. *Proverbs 18:24*

He hath said, I will never leave thee, nor forsake thee. *Hebrews 13:5*

Godly

But know that the LORD hath set apart him that is godly for himself: the LORD will hear when I call unto him. *Psalm 4:3*

And to knowledge temperance; and to temperance patience; and to patience godliness; And to godliness brotherly kindness; and to brotherly kindness charity. For if these things be in you, and abound, they make *you that ye shall* neither *be* barren nor unfruitful in the knowledge of our Lord Jesus Christ. *2 Peter 1:6-8*

The LORD knoweth the days of the upright: their inheritance shall be forever. They shall not be ashamed in the evil time: in the days of famine they shall be satisfied. *Psalm 37:18-19*

The steps of a *good* man are ordered by the
LORD: and he delighteth in his way. Though
he fall, he shall not be utterly cast down: for
the LORD upholdeth *him with* his hand.

Psalm 37:23-24

When a man's ways please the LORD, he
maketh even his enemies to be at peace with
him.   *Proverbs 16:7*

Light is sown for the righteous, and gladness
for the upright in heart.   *Psalm 97:11*

The Lord knoweth how to deliver the godly
out of temptations.   *2 Peter 2:9*

But godliness with contentment is great gain.
1 Timothy 6:6

O continue thy lovingkindness unto them that
know thee; and thy righteousness to the upright in heart.   *Psalm 36:10*

My defense *is* of God, which saveth the upright in heart.   *Psalm 7:10*

Godliness is profitable unto all things, having
promise of the life that now is, and of that
which is to come.   *1 Timothy 4:8*

Guilty

I, *even* I, *am* he that blotteth out thy transgressions for mine own sake, and will not remember thy sins. *Isaiah 43:25*

Blessed *is he whose* transgression *is* forgiven,
whose sin *is* covered. Blessed *is* the man unto
whom the LORD imputeth not iniquity, and in
whose spirit *there is* no guile. *Psalm 32:1-2*

For I will be merciful to their unrighteousness, and their sins and their iniquities will I
remember no more. *Hebrews 8:12*

For God sent not his Son into the world to
condemn the world; but that the world
through him might be saved. He that believeth on him is not condemned: but he that
believeth not is condemned already, because
he hath not believed in the name of the only
begotten Son of God. *John 3:17-18*

Be it known unto you therefore, men *and*
brethren, that through this man is preached
unto you the forgiveness of sins: And by him
all that believe are justified from all things,
from which ye could not be justified by the
law of Moses. *Acts 13:38-39*

There is therefore now no condemnation to them which are in Christ Jesus, who walk not after the flesh, but after the Spirit. For the law of the Spirit of life in Christ Jesus hath made me free from the law of sin and death.

Romans 8:1-2

He hath not dealt with us after our sins; nor rewarded us according to our iniquities. For as the heaven is high above the earth, *so* great is his mercy toward them that fear him. As far as the east is from the west, *so* far hath he removed our transgressions from us.

Psalm 103:10-12

Let the wicked forsake his way, and the unrighteous man his thoughts: and let him return unto the LORD, and he will have mercy upon him; and to our God, for he will abundantly pardon.   *Isaiah 55:7*

For if our heart condemn us, God is greater than our heart, and knoweth all things.   *1 John 3:20*

How much more shall the blood of Christ, who through the eternal Spirit offered himself without spot to God, purge your conscience from dead works to serve the living God?

Hebrews 9:14

If we confess our sins, he is faithful and just to forgive us *our* sins, and to cleanse us from all unrighteousness.   *1 John 1:9*

Helpless

For I the LORD thy God will hold thy right hand, saying unto thee, Fear not; I will help thee.   *Isaiah 41:13*

The poor committeth himself unto thee; thou art the helper of the fatherless.   *Psalm 10:14*

He shall deliver thee in six troubles: yea, in seven there shall no evil touch thee.   *Job 5:19*

The LORD also will be a refuge for the oppressed, a refuge in times of trouble.   *Psalm 9:9*

And he said unto me, My grace is sufficient for thee: for my strength is made perfect in weakness.   *2 Corinthians 12:9*

Likewise the Spirit also helpeth our infirmities: for we know not what we should pray for as we ought: but the Spirit itself maketh intercession for us with groanings which cannot be uttered.   *Romans 8:26*

Let us therefore come boldly unto the throne of grace, that we may obtain mercy, and find grace to help in time of need.   *Hebrews 4:16*

God *is* mine helper: the Lord *is* with them that uphold my soul.   *Psalm 54:4*

I can do all things through Christ which strengtheneth me.   *Philippians 4:13*

So that we may boldly say, The Lord *is* my helper, and I will not fear what man shall do unto me.   *Hebrews 13:6*

Greater is he that is in you, than he that is in the world.   *1 John 4:4*

Honest

Keep thy heart with all diligence; for out of it *are* the issues of life. Put away from thee a froward mouth, and perverse lips put far from thee.   *Proverbs 4:23-24*

LORD, who shall abide in thy tabernacle? who shall dwell in thy holy hill? He that walketh uprightly, and worketh righteousness, and speaketh the truth in his heart. *Psalm 15:1-2*

Lying lips *are* abomination to the LORD: but they that deal truly *are* his delight.

Proverbs 12:22

The wicked is snared by the transgression of *his* lips: but the just shall come out of trouble.

Proverbs 12:13

Who shall ascend into the hill of the LORD? or who shall stand in his holy place? He that hath clean hands, and a pure heart; who hath not lifted up his soul unto vanity, nor sworn deceitfully. He shall receive the blessing from the LORD, and righteousness from the God of his salvation.

Psalm 24:3-5

He that walketh righteously, and speaketh uprightly; he that despiseth the gain of oppressions, that shaketh his hands from holding of bribes...He shall dwell on high...bread shall be given him; his waters *shall be* sure. Thine eyes shall see the king in his beauty: they shall behold the land that is very far off.

Isaiah 33:15-17

What man *is he that* desireth life, *and* loveth *many* days, that he may see good? Keep thy tongue from evil, and thy lips from speaking guile.

Psalm 34:12-13

The lip of truth shall be established for ever: but a lying tongue *is* but for a moment.

Proverbs 12:19

A man shall be satisfied with good by the fruit of *his* mouth.   *Proverbs 12:14*

Impatient

Wait on the LORD: be of good courage, and he shall strengthen thine heart: wait, I say, on the LORD.   *Psalm 27:14*

Rest in the LORD, and wait patiently for him: fret not thyself because of him who prospereth in his way.   *Psalm 37:7*

Cast not away therefore your confidence, which hath great recompense of reward. For ye have need of patience, that, after ye have done the will of God, ye might receive the promise.   *Hebrews 10:35-36*

Knowing *this,* that the trying of your faith worketh patience. But let patience have *her* perfect work, that ye may be perfect and entire, wanting nothing.   *James 1:3-4*

Wait on the LORD, and keep his way, and he shall exalt thee to inherit the land.

Psalm 37:34

That ye be not slothful, but followers of them who through faith and patience inherit the promises.   *Hebrews 6:12*

And not only *so,* but we glory in tribulations also: knowing that tribulation worketh patience; And patience, experience; and experience, hope: And hope maketh not ashamed; because the love of God is shed abroad in our hearts by the Holy Ghost which is given unto us.   *Romans 5:3-5*

Lonely

For he hath said, I will never leave thee, nor forsake thee.   *Hebrews 13:5*

I the LORD have called thee in righteousness, and will hold thine hand, and will keep thee.

Isaiah 42:6

God setteth the solitary in families: he bringeth out those which are bound with chains.   *Psalm 68:6*

I will not leave you comfortless: I will come to you. *John 14:18*

For the mountains shall depart, and the hills be removed; but my kindness shall not depart from thee, neither shall the covenant of my peace be removed, saith the LORD that hath mercy on thee. *Isaiah 54:10*

When my father and my mother forsake me, then the LORD will take me up. *Psalm 27:10*

When thou passest through the waters, I *will be* with thee; and through the rivers, they shall not overflow thee: when thou walkest through the fire, thou shalt not be burned; neither shall the flame kindle upon thee...Fear not: for I *am* with thee. *Isaiah 43:2, 5*

Lo, I am with you alway, *even* unto the end of the world. *Matthew 28:20*

Persecuted

And ye shall be hated of all *men* for my name's sake. But there shall not an hair of your head perish. In your patience possess ye your souls. *Luke 21:17-19*

Blessed are ye, when *men* shall revile you, and persecute *you,* and shall say all manner of evil against you falsely, for my sake. Rejoice, and be exceeding glad: for great *is* your reward in heaven: for so persecuted they the prophets which were before you. *Matthew 5:11-12*

But before all these, they shall lay their hands on you, and persecute *you,* delivering *you* up to the synagogues, and into prisons, being brought before kings and rulers for my name's sake. And it shall turn to you for a testimony. Settle *it* therefore in your hearts, not to meditate before what ye shall answer: For I will give you a mouth and wisdom, which all your adversaries shall not be able to gainsay nor resist. *Luke 21:12-15*

Love your enemies, bless them that curse you, do good to them that hate you, and pray for them which despitefully use you, and persecute you; That ye may be the children of your Father which is in heaven.

Matthew 5:44-45

We are troubled on every side, yet not distressed; *we are* perplexed, but not in despair; Persecuted, but not forsaken; cast down, but not destroyed. *2 Corinthians 4:8-9*

It is a faithful saying: For if we be dead with *him,* we shall also live with *him:* If we suffer, we shall also reign with *him.*   *2 Timothy 2:11-12*

Blessed *are* they which are persecuted for righteousness' sake: for theirs is the kingdom of heaven.   *Matthew 5:10*

Personally Attacked

Fear ye not, stand still, and see the salvation of the LORD, which he will show to you to day...The LORD shall fight for you, and ye shall hold your peace.   *Exodus 14:13-14*

But the salvation of the righteous *is* of the LORD: *he is* their strength in the time of trouble. And the LORD shall help them, and deliver them: he shall deliver them from the wicked, and save them, because they trust in him.   *Psalm 37:39-40*

The LORD *is* my light and my salvation; whom shall I fear? the LORD *is* the strength of my life; of whom shall I be afraid? When the wicked, *even* mine enemies and my foes, came upon me to eat up my flesh, they stumbled and fell.   *Psalm 27:1-2*

Not rendering evil for evil, or railing for railing: but contrariwise blessing; knowing that ye are thereunto called, that ye should inherit a blessing. *1 Peter 3:9*

Dearly beloved, avenge not yourselves, but *rather* give place unto wrath: for it is written, Vengeance *is* mine; I will repay, saith the Lord. Therefore if thine enemy hunger, feed him; if he thirst, give him drink: for in so doing thou shalt heap coals of fire on his head. Be not overcome of evil, but overcome evil with good. *Romans 12:19-21*

But let all those that put their trust in thee rejoice: let them ever shout for joy, because thou defendest them. *Psalm 5:11*

And they shall fight against thee, but they shall not prevail against thee: for I *am* with thee to save thee and to deliver thee, saith the LORD. *Jeremiah 15:20*

And I will deliver thee out of the hand of the wicked, and I will redeem thee out of the hand of the terrible. *Jeremiah 15:21*

What shall we then say to these things? If God *be* for us, who *can be* against us? *Romans 8:31*

Righteous

For thou, LORD, wilt bless the righteous; with favor wilt thou compass him as *with* a shield.
Psalm 5:12

He layeth up sound wisdom for the righteous: *he is* a buckler to them that walk uprightly. He keepeth the paths of judgment, and preserveth the way of his saints.   *Proverbs 2:7-8*

The desire of the righteous shall be granted.
Proverbs 10:24

He withdraweth not his eyes from the righteous: but with kings *are they* on the throne; yea, he doth establish them for ever, and they are exalted.   *Job 36:7*

The eyes of the LORD *are* upon the righteous, and his ears *are open* unto their cry...*The righteous* cry, and the LORD heareth, and delivereth them out of all their troubles...Many *are* the afflictions of the righteous: but the LORD delivereth him out of them all.   *Psalm 34:15, 17, 19*

The righteous also shall hold on his way, and he that hath clean hands shall be stronger and stronger.   *Job 17:9*

The hope of the righteous *shall be* gladness ...The way of the LORD *is* strength to the upright. *Proverbs 10:28-29*

The righteous *is* an everlasting foundation ...The righteous shall never be removed.
Proverbs 10:25, 30

I have been young, and *now* am old; yet have I not seen the righteous forsaken, nor his seed begging bread...The righteous shall inherit the land, and dwell therein forever. *Psalm 37:25, 29*

They which receive abundance of grace and of the gift of righteousness shall reign in life by one, Jesus Christ. *Romans 5:17*

Then shall the righteous shine forth as the sun in the kingdom of their Father. *Matthew 13:43*

The LORD loveth the righteous. *Psalm 146:8*

Sick

And the LORD will take away from thee all sickness, and will put none of the evil diseases of Egypt, which thou knowest, upon thee.
Deuteronomy 7:15

Blessed *is* he that considereth the poor: the
LORD will deliver him in time of trouble...The
LORD will strengthen him upon the bed of
languishing: thou wilt make all his bed in his
sickness.   *Psalm 41:1, 3*

Is any sick among you? let him call for the el-
ders of the church; and let them pray over
him, anointing him with oil in the name of the
Lord: And the prayer of faith shall save the
sick, and the Lord shall raise him up; and if he
have committed sins, they shall be forgiven
him.   *James 5:14-15*

And these signs shall follow them that believe;
In my name shall they cast out devils; they
shall speak with new tongues...they shall lay
hands on the sick, and they shall recover.
                                      Mark 16:17-18

As many as touched [the hem of his garment]
were made perfectly whole.   *Matthew 14:36*

He cast out the spirits with *his* word, and
healed all that were sick: That it might be
fulfilled which was spoken by Esaias the
prophet, saying, Himself took our infirmities,
and bare *our* sicknesses.   *Matthew 8:16-17*

I will take sickness away from the midst of thee. *Exodus 23:25*

Sorrowful

Blessed *are* they that mourn: for they shall be comforted. *Matthew 5:4*

Then shall the virgin rejoice in the dance, both young men and old together: for I will turn their mourning into joy, and will comfort them, and make them rejoice from their sorrow. *Jeremiah 31:13*

Ye now therefore have sorrow: but I will see you again, and your heart shall rejoice, and your joy no man taketh from you. *John 16:22*

They that sow in tears shall reap in joy. He that goeth forth and weepeth, bearing precious seed, shall doubtless come again with rejoicing, bringing his sheaves *with him.*
Psalm 126:5-6

Sing, O heavens; and be joyful, O earth; and break forth into singing, O mountains: for the LORD hath comforted his people, and will have mercy upon his afflicted. *Isaiah 49:13*

Therefore the redeemed of the LORD shall return, and come with singing unto Zion; and everlasting joy *shall be* upon their head: they shall obtain gladness and joy; *and* sorrow and mourning shall flee away.   *Isaiah 51:11*

Weeping may endure for a night, but joy cometh in the morning.   *Psalm 30:5*

And God shall wipe away all tears from their eyes; and there shall be no more death, neither sorrow, nor crying, neither shall there be any more pain: for the former things are passed away.   *Revelation 21:4*

Tempted

Blessed is the man that endureth temptation: for when he is tried, he shall receive the crown of life, which the Lord hath promised to them that love him.   *James 1:12*

Abstain from all appearance of evil. And the very God of peace sanctify you wholly; I pray God your whole spirit and soul and body be preserved blameless unto the coming of our Lord Jesus Christ. Faithful is he that calleth you, who also will do it.   *1 Thessalonians 5:22-24*

And delivered just Lot, vexed with the filthy conversation of the wicked: (For that righteous man dwelling among them, in seeing and hearing, vexed his righteous soul from day to day with their unlawful deeds;) The Lord knoweth how to deliver the godly out of temptations.
2 Peter 2:7-9

Seeing then that we have a great high priest, that is passed into the heavens, Jesus the Son of God, let us hold fast our profession. For we have not an high priest which cannot be touched with the feeling of our infirmities; but was in all points tempted like as we are, yet without sin. Let us therefore come boldly unto the throne of grace, that we may obtain mercy, and find grace to help in time of need.
Hebrews 4:14-16

For in that he himself hath suffered being tempted, he is able to succor them that are tempted.
Hebrews 2:18

There hath no temptation taken you but such as is common to man: but God is faithful, who will not suffer you to be tempted above that ye are able; but will with the temptation also make a way to escape, that ye may be able to bear it.
1 Corinthians 10:13

Under Satanic Attack

Submit yourselves therefore to God. Resist the devil, and he will flee from you. *James 4:7*

Fear none of those things which thou shalt suffer: behold, the devil shall cast *some* of you into prison...be thou faithful unto death, and I will give thee a crown of life. *Revelation 2:10*

We know that whosoever is born of God sinneth not; but he that is begotten of God keepeth himself, and that wicked one toucheth him not.   *1 John 5:18*

Grace be to you and peace from God the Father, and from our Lord Jesus Christ, Who gave himself for our sins, that he might deliver us from this present evil world, according to the will of God and our Father.   *Galatians 1:3-4*

I pray not that thou shouldest take them out of the world, but that thou shouldest keep them from the evil. They are not of the world, even as I am not of the world.   *John 17:15-16*

And the God of peace shall bruise Satan under your feet shortly. The grace of our Lord Jesus Christ *be* with you.   *Romans 16:20*

Worried

Be careful for nothing; but in every thing by prayer and supplication with thanksgiving let your requests be made known unto God. And the peace of God, which passeth all understanding, shall keep your hearts and minds through Christ Jesus.   *Philippians 4:6-7*

Therefore take no thought, saying, What shall we eat? or, What shall we drink? or, Wherewithal shall we be clothed? (For after all these things do the Gentiles seek:) for your heavenly Father knoweth that ye have need of all these things. But seek ye first the kingdom of God, and his righteousness; and all these things shall be added unto you.

Matthew 6:31-33

Better *is* an handful *with* quietness, than both the hands full *with* travail and vexation of spirit.   *Ecclesiastes 4:6*

Take therefore no thought for the morrow: for the morrow shall take thought for the things of itself.   *Matthew 6:34*

In the multitude of my thoughts within me thy comforts delight my soul.   *Psalm 94:19*

And which of you with taking thought can add
to his stature one cubit? If ye then be not able
to do that thing which is least, why take ye
thought for the rest?   *Luke 12:25-26*

Fret not thyself because of evildoers, neither
be thou envious against the workers of iniquity. For they shall soon be cut down like the
grass, and wither as the green herb. Trust in
the LORD, and do good; *so* shalt thou dwell in
the land, and verily thou shalt be fed. Delight
thyself also in the LORD; and he shall give
thee the desires of thine heart. Commit thy
way unto the LORD; trust also in him; and he
shall bring *it* to pass...Rest in the LORD, and
wait patiently for him: fret not thyself because
of him who prospereth in his way, because of
the man who bringeth wicked devices to pass.
                                   Psalm 37:1-5, 7

Not that I speak in respect of want: for I have
learned, in whatsoever state I am, *therewith* to
be content...I can do all things through Christ
which strengtheneth me. *Philippians 4:11, 13*

Hear me when I call, O God of my righteousness: thou hast enlarged me *when I was* in
distress; have mercy upon me, and hear my
prayer.   *Psalm 4:1*

Though I walk in the midst of trouble, thou wilt revive me: thou shalt stretch forth thine hand against the wrath of mine enemies, and thy right hand shall save me. The LORD will perfect *that which* concerneth me: thy mercy, O LORD, *endureth* for ever: forsake not the works of thine own hands.   *Psalm 138:7-8*

In my distress I called upon the LORD, and cried unto my God: he heard my voice out of his temple, and my cry came before him, *even* into his ears.   *Psalm 18:6*

When your fear cometh as desolation, and your destruction cometh as a whirlwind; when distress and anguish cometh upon you...But whoso hearkeneth unto me shall dwell safely, and shall be quiet from fear of evil.

Proverbs 1:27, 33

Humble yourselves therefore under the mighty hand of God, that he may exalt you in due time: Casting all your care upon him; for he careth for you.   *1 Peter 5:6-7*

Bible Promises for Those Who...

Believe in Jesus Christ

Whosoever believeth that Jesus is the Christ is born of God: and every one that loveth him that begat loveth him also that is begotten of him.

1 John 5:1

He that believeth on me, as the scripture hath said, out of his belly shall flow rivers of living water.

John 7:38

Who is he that overcometh the world, but he that believeth that Jesus is the Son of God?

1 John 5:5

And Jesus said unto them, I am the bread of life: he that cometh to me shall never hunger; and he that believeth on me shall never thirst. ...And this is the will of him that sent me, that every one which seeth the Son, and believeth on him, may have everlasting life: and I will raise him up at the last day.   *John 6:35, 40*

For we which have believed do enter into rest.
                                          Hebrews 4:3

Verily, verily, I say unto you, He that heareth my word, and believeth on him that sent me, hath everlasting life, and shall not come into condemnation; but is passed from death unto life.   *John 5:24*

To him give all the prophets witness, that through his name whosoever believeth in him shall receive remission of sins.   *Acts 10:43*

Verily, verily, I say unto you, He that believeth on me, the works that I do shall he do also; and greater *works* than these shall he do; because I go unto my Father.   *John 14:12*

I am come a light into the world, that whosoever believeth on me should not abide in darkness.   *John 12:46*

And whosoever liveth and believeth in me
shall never die. *John 11:26*

But to him that worketh not, but believeth on
him that justifieth the ungodly, his faith is
counted for righteousness. *Romans 4:5*

Whosoever believeth on him shall not be
ashamed. *Romans 9:33*

Jesus said unto him, If thou canst believe, all
things *are* possible to him that believeth.
Mark 9:23

Do Good Deeds

Blessed *is* he that considereth the poor: the
LORD will deliver him in time of trouble.
Psalm 41:1

And whosoever shall give to drink unto one of
these little ones a cup of cold *water* only in the
name of a disciple, verily I say unto you, he
shall in no wise lose his reward. *Matthew 10:42*

He that hath pity upon the poor lendeth unto
the LORD; and that which he hath given will
he pay him again. *Proverbs 19:17*

Is it not to deal thy bread to the hungry, and that thou bring the poor that are cast out to thy house? when thou seest the naked, that thou cover him; and that thou hide not thyself from thine own flesh? Then shall thy light break forth as the morning, and thine health shall spring forth speedily: and thy righteousness shall go before thee; the glory of the LORD shall be thy reward. Then shalt thou call, and the LORD shall answer; thou shalt cry, and he shall say, Here I *am*. If thou take away from the midst of thee the yoke, the putting forth of the finger, and speaking vanity; And *if* thou draw out thy soul to the hungry, and satisfy the afflicted soul; then shall thy light rise in obscurity, and thy darkness *be* as the noon day: And the LORD shall guide thee continually, and satisfy thy soul in drought, and make fat thy bones: and thou shalt be like a watered garden, and like a spring of water, whose waters fail not. *Isaiah 58:7-11*

And let us not be weary in well doing: for in due season we shall reap, if we faint not.
Galatians 6:9

For God *is* not unrighteous to forget your work and labor of love, which ye have showed toward his name, in that ye have ministered to the saints, and do minister. *Hebrews 6:10*

Let your light so shine before men, that they may see your good works, and glorify your Father which is in heaven.   *Matthew 5:16*

Charge them that are rich in this world, that they be not high-minded, nor trust in uncertain riches, but in the living God, who giveth us richly all things to enjoy; That they do good, that they be rich in good works, ready to distribute, willing to communicate; Laying up in store for themselves a good foundation against the time to come, that they may lay hold on eternal life.   *1 Timothy 6:17-19*

For I was an hungered, and ye gave me meat: I was thirsty, and ye gave me drink: I was a stranger, and ye took me in: Naked, and ye clothed me: I was sick, and ye visited me: I was in prison, and ye came unto me. Then shall the righteous answer him, saying, Lord, when saw we thee an hungered, and fed *thee?* or thirsty, and gave *thee* drink? When saw we thee a stranger, and took *thee* in? or naked, and clothed *thee?* Or when saw we thee sick, or in prison, and came unto thee? And the King shall answer and say unto them, Verily I say unto you, Inasmuch as ye have done *it* unto one of the least of these my brethren, ye have done *it* unto me.   *Matthew 25:35-40*

Thou shalt surely give him [someone in need],
and thine heart shall not be grieved when
thou givest unto him: because that for this
thing the LORD thy God shall bless thee in all
thy works, and in all that thou puttest thine
hand unto. For the poor shall never cease out
of the land: therefore I command thee, saying,
Thou shalt open thine hand wide unto thy
brother, to thy poor, and to thy needy, in thy
land.					*Deuteronomy 15:10-11*

Who can find a virtuous woman? for her price
is far above rubies...She stretcheth out her
hand to the poor; yea, she reacheth forth her
hands to the needy...Strength and honor *are*
her clothing; and she shall rejoice in time to
come...Her children arise up, and call her
blessed; her husband *also,* and he praiseth
her.					*Proverbs 31:10, 20, 25, 28*

Hereby perceive we the love *of God,* because
he laid down his life for us: and we ought to
lay down *our* lives for the brethren. But whoso
hath this world's good, and seeth his brother
have need, and shutteth up his bowels *of compassion* from him, how dwelleth the love of
God in him? My little children, let us not love
in word, neither in tongue; but in deed and in
truth.					*1 John 3:16-18*

And the people asked him, saying, What shall we do then? He answereth and saith unto them, He that hath two coats, let him impart to him that hath none; and he that hath meat, let him do likewise.   *Luke 3:10-11*

For we are his workmanship, created in Christ Jesus unto good works, which God hath before ordained that we should walk in them.

Ephesians 2:10

Endure Trials and Tribulations

My brethren, count it all joy when ye fall into divers temptations. Knowing *this,* that the trying of your faith worketh patience. But let patience have *her* perfect work, that ye may be perfect and entire, wanting nothing.

James 1:2-4

These things I have spoken unto you, that in me ye might have peace. In the world ye shall have tribulation: but be of good cheer; I have overcome the world.   *John 16:33*

And not only *so,* but we glory in tribulations also: knowing that tribulation worketh patience.   *Romans 5:3*

To an inheritance incorruptible, and undefiled, and that fadeth not away, reserved in heaven for you, Who are kept by the power of God through faith unto salvation ready to be revealed in the last time. Wherein ye greatly rejoice, though now for a season, if need be, ye are in heaviness through manifold temptations, That the trial of your faith, being much more precious than of gold that perisheth, though it be tried with fire, might be found unto praise and honor and glory at the appearing of Jesus Christ.   *1 Peter 1:4-7*

But the salvation of the righteous *is* of the LORD: *he is* their strength in the time of trouble. And the LORD shall help them, and deliver them: he shall deliver them from the wicked, and save them, because they trust in him.   *Psalm 37:39-40*

Many *are* the afflictions of the righteous: but the LORD delivereth him out of them all.
                                        Psalm 34:19

Because he hath set his love upon me, therefore will I deliver him...He shall call upon me, and I will answer him: I *will be* with him in trouble; I will deliver him, and honor him.
                                        Psalm 91:14-15

So that we ourselves glory in you in the churches of God for your patience and faith in all your persecutions and tribulations that ye endure: *Which is* a manifest token of the righteous judgment of God, that ye may be counted worthy of the kingdom of God, for which ye also suffer...When he shall come to be glorified in his saints, and to be admired in all them that believe (because our testimony among you was believed) in that day. Wherefore also we pray always for you, that our God would count you worthy of *this* calling, and fulfill all the good pleasure of *his* goodness, and the work of faith with power. That the name of our Lord Jesus Christ may be glorified in you, and ye in him, according to the grace of our God and the Lord Jesus Christ.

2 Thessalonians 1:4-5, 10-12

When thou passest through the waters, I *will be* with thee; and through the rivers, they shall not overflow thee: when thou walkest through the fire, thou shalt not be burned; neither shall the flame kindle upon thee. For I *am* the LORD thy God, the Holy One of Israel, thy Savior.   *Isaiah 43:2-3*

God *is* our refuge and strength, a very present help in trouble.   *Psalm 46:1*

Fear the Lord

But in every nation he that feareth him, and worketh righteousness, is accepted with him.

Acts 10:35

Blessed *is* the man *that* feareth the LORD, *that* delighteth greatly in his commandments. His seed shall be mighty upon earth: the generation of the upright shall be blessed. Wealth and riches *shall be* in his house: and his righteousness endureth for ever.   *Psalm 112:1-3*

In the fear of the LORD *is* strong confidence: and his children shall have a place of refuge. The fear of the LORD *is* a fountain of life, to depart from the snares of death.

Proverbs 14:26-27

Oh how great *is* thy goodness, which thou hast laid up for them that fear thee; *which* thou hast wrought for them that trust in thee before the sons of men!   *Psalm 31:19*

The angel of the LORD encampeth round about them that fear him, and delivereth them...O fear the LORD, ye his saints: for *there is* no want to them that fear him.

Psalm 34:7, 9

Ye that fear the LORD, trust in the LORD: he *is* their help and their shield. The LORD hath been mindful of us: he will bless *us;* he will bless the house of Israel; he will bless the house of Aaron. He will bless them that fear the LORD, *both* small and great. The LORD shall increase you more and more, you and your children.   *Psalm 115:11-14*

What man *is* he that feareth the LORD? him shall he teach in the way *that* he shall choose. His soul shall dwell at ease; and his seed shall inherit the earth.   *Psalm 25:12-13*

Blessed *is* every one that feareth the LORD; that walketh in his ways. For thou shalt eat the labor of thine hands: happy *shalt* thou *be,* and *it shall be* well with thee.   *Psalm 128:1-2*

Behold, the eye of the LORD *is* upon them that fear him, upon them that hope in his mercy.
          Psalm 33:18

Like as a father pitieth *his* children, *so* the LORD pitieth them that fear him.   *Psalm 103:13*

The fear of the LORD prolongeth days: but the years of the wicked shall be shortened.
          Proverbs 10:27

And the LORD commanded us to do all these statutes, to fear the LORD our God, for our good always, that he might preserve us alive, as *it is* at this day.   *Deuteronomy 6:24*

For as the heaven is high above the earth, *so* great is his mercy toward them that fear him.
                                              Psalm 103:11

Give to Others

And God *is* able to make all grace abound toward you; that ye, always having all sufficiency in all *things,* may abound to every good work.   *2 Corinthians 9:8*

Honor the LORD with thy substance, and with the firstfruits of all thine increase: So shall thy barns be filled with plenty, and thy presses shall burst out with new wine.
                                              Proverbs 3:9-10

Give, and it shall be given unto you; good measure, pressed down, and shaken together, and running over, shall men give into your bosom. For with the same measure that ye mete withal it shall be measured to you again.
                                              Luke 6:38

Remember the words of the Lord Jesus, how he said, It is more blessed to give than to receive.
Acts 20:35

And he which soweth sparingly shall reap also sparingly; and he which soweth bountifully shall reap also bountifully.
2 Corinthians 9:6

The liberal soul shall be made fat: and he that watereth shall be watered also himself.
Proverbs 11:25

Every man according as he purposeth in his heart, *so let him give;* not grudgingly, or of necessity: for God loveth a cheerful giver.
2 Corinthians 9:7

He that giveth unto the poor shall not lack.
Proverbs 28:27

Bring ye all the tithes into the storehouse, that there may be meat in mine house, and prove me now herewith, saith the LORD of hosts, if I will not open you the windows of heaven, and pour you out a blessing, that *there shall* not *be room* enough *to receive it.*
Malachi 3:10

Love God

Because he hath set his love upon me, therefore will I deliver him: I will set him on high, because he hath known my name. He shall call upon me, and I will answer him: I *will be* with him in trouble; I will deliver him, and honor him.   *Psalm 91:14-15*

And we know that all things work together for good to them that love God, to them who are the called according to *his* purpose.
Romans 8:28

Blessed *is* the man that endureth temptation: for when he is tried, he shall receive the crown of life, which the Lord hath promised to them that love him.   *James 1:12*

Know therefore that the LORD thy God, he *is* God, the faithful God, which keepeth covenant and mercy with them that love him and keep his commandments to a thousand generations.   *Deuteronomy 7:9*

If a man love me, he will keep my words: and my Father will love him, and we will come unto him, and make our abode with him.
John 14:23

The LORD preserveth all them that love him: but all the wicked will he destroy.

Psalm 145:20

But if any man love God, the same is known of him.   *1 Corinthians 8:3*

It is written, Eye hath not seen, nor ear heard, neither have entered into the heart of man, the things which God hath prepared for them that love him.   *1 Corinthians 2:9*

Obey the Lord

Blessed *are* they that hear the word of God, and keep it.   *Luke 11:28*

He that hath my commandments, and keepeth them, he it is that loveth me: and he that loveth me shall be loved of my Father, and I will love him, and will manifest myself to him.

John 14:21

And hereby we do know that we know him, if we keep his commandments...But whoso keepeth his word, in him verily is the love of God perfected: hereby know we that we are in him.   *1 John 2:3, 5*

Whosoever therefore shall break one of these least commandments, and shall teach men so, he shall be called the least in the kingdom of heaven: but whosoever shall do and teach *them,* the same shall be called great in the kingdom of heaven.   *Matthew 5:19*

Ye are my friends, if ye do whatsoever I command you.   *John 15:14*

Hear therefore, O Israel, and observe to do *it;* that it may be well with thee, and that ye may increase mightily, as the LORD God of thy fathers hath promised thee, in the land that floweth with milk and honey...And thou shalt do *that which is* right and good in the sight of the LORD: that it may be well with thee, and that thou mayest go in and possess the good land which the LORD sware unto thy fathers.
Deuteronomy 6:3, 18

See, I have set before thee this day life and good, and death and evil. In that I command thee this day to love the LORD thy God, to walk in his ways, and to keep his commandments and his statutes and his judgments, that thou mayest live and multiply: and the LORD thy God shall bless thee in the land whither thou goest to possess it.   *Deuteronomy 30:15-16*

For whosoever shall do the will of my Father
which is in heaven, the same is my brother,
and sister, and mother.   *Matthew 12:50*

And the world passeth away, and the lust
thereof: but he that doeth the will of God abideth for ever.   *1 John 2:17*

All the paths of the LORD *are* mercy and truth
unto such as keep his covenant and his testimonies.   *Psalm 25:10*

Pray

Be careful for nothing; but in every thing by
prayer and supplication with thanksgiving let
your requests be made known unto God. And
the peace of God, which passeth all understanding, shall keep your hearts and minds
through Christ Jesus.   *Philippians 4:6-7*

If my people, which are called by my name,
shall humble themselves, and pray, and seek
my face, and turn from their wicked ways;
then will I hear from heaven, and will forgive
their sin, and will heal their land.

2 Chronicles 7:14

But thou, when thou prayest, enter into thy closet, and when thou hast shut thy door, pray to thy Father which is in secret; and thy Father which seeth in secret shall reward thee openly.   *Matthew 6:6*

And the prayer of faith shall save the sick, and the Lord shall raise him up; and if he have committed sins, they shall be forgiven him. The effectual fervent prayer of a righteous man availeth much.   *James 5:15-16*

But ye, beloved, building up yourselves on your most holy faith, praying in the Holy Ghost.   *Jude 20*

If ye abide in me, and my words abide in you, ye shall ask what ye will, and it shall be done unto you. Herein is my Father glorified, that ye bear much fruit; so shall ye be my disciples.
                                              John 15:7-8

Ask, and it shall be given you; seek, and ye shall find; knock, and it shall be opened unto you: For every one that asketh receiveth; and he that seeketh findeth; and to him that knocketh it shall be opened.
                                            Matthew 7:7-8

Seek the Lord

But seek ye first the kingdom of God, and his righteousness; and all these things shall be added unto you. *Matthew 6:33*

But if from thence thou shalt seek the LORD thy God, thou shalt find *him,* if thou seek him with all thy heart and with all thy soul.
Deuteronomy 4:29

Let all those that seek thee rejoice and be glad in thee: and let such as love thy salvation say continually, Let God be magnified. *Psalm 70:4*

I sought the LORD, and he heard me, and delivered me from all my fears...The young lions do lack, and suffer hunger: but they that seek the LORD shall not want any good *thing*.
Psalm 34:4,10

I love them that love me; and those that seek me early shall find me. *Proverbs 8:17*

And ye shall seek me, and find *me,* when ye shall search for me with all your heart. And I will be found of you, saith the LORD.
Jeremiah 29:13-14

The humble shall see *this, and* be glad: your
heart shall live that seek God.   *Psalm 69:32*

But without faith *it is* impossible to please
him: for he that cometh to God must believe
that he is, and *that* he is a rewarder of them
that diligently seek him.   *Hebrews 11:6*

Serve God

And whatsoever ye do, do *it* heartily, as to the
Lord, and not unto men; Knowing that of the
Lord ye shall receive the reward of the inheri-
tance: for ye serve the Lord Christ.
                              Colossians 3:23-24

If any man serve me, let him follow me; and
where I am, there shall also my servant be: if
any man serve me, him will *my* Father honor.
                                   John 12:26

The LORD redeemeth the soul of his servants:
and none of them that trust in him shall be
desolate.   *Psalm 34:22*

If they obey and serve *him,* they shall spend
their days in prosperity, and their years in
pleasures.   *Job 36:11*

Therefore, my beloved brethren, be ye stedfast, unmoveable, always abounding in the work of the Lord, forasmuch as ye know that your labor is not in vain in the Lord.   *1 Corinthians 15:58*

Present your bodies a living sacrifice, holy, acceptable unto God, *which is* your reasonable service. And be not conformed to this world: but be ye transformed by the renewing of your mind, that ye may prove what *is* that good, and acceptable, and perfect, will of God.
Romans 12:1-2

Serve the LORD with gladness...For the LORD *is* good; his mercy *is* everlasting; and his truth *endureth* to all generations.   *Psalm 100:2, 5*

And there shall be no more curse: but the throne of God and of the Lamb shall be in it; and his servants shall serve him: And they shall see his face; and his name *shall be* in their foreheads.   *Revelation 22:3-4*

Suffer for Christ

For our light affliction, which is but for a moment, worketh for us a far more exceeding *and* eternal weight of glory.   *2 Corinthians 4:17*

If so be that we suffer with *him,* that we may be also glorified together. For I reckon that the sufferings of this present time *are* not worthy *to be compared* with the glory which shall be revealed in us.   *Romans 8:17-18*

And our hope of you *is* stedfast, knowing, that as ye are partakers of the sufferings, so *shall ye be* also of the consolation. *2 Corinthians 1:7*

And he said to *them* all, If any *man* will come after me, let him deny himself, and take up his cross daily, and follow me. For whosoever will save his life shall lose it: but whosoever will lose his life for my sake, the same shall save it.   *Luke 9:23-24*

For what glory *is it,* if, when ye be buffeted for your faults, ye shall take it patiently? but if, when ye do well, and suffer *for it,* ye take it patiently, this *is* acceptable with God.

1 Peter 2:20

Which is a manifest token of the righteous judgment of God, that ye may be counted worthy of the kingdom of God, for which ye also suffer: Seeing *it is* a righteous thing with God to recompense tribulation to them that trouble you.   *2 Thessalonians 1:5-6*

But the God of all grace, who hath called us unto his eternal glory by Christ Jesus, after that ye have suffered a while, make you perfect, stablish, strengthen, settle *you*.   *1 Peter 5:10*

If ye be reproached for the name of Christ, happy *are ye;* for the spirit of glory and of God resteth upon you: on their part he is evil spoken of, but on your part he is glorified.
1 Peter 4:14

Trust the Lord

Trust in the LORD with all thine heart; and lean not unto thine own understanding. In all thy ways acknowledge him, and he shall direct thy paths.   *Proverbs 3:5-6*

For our heart shall rejoice in him, because we have trusted in his holy name. Let thy mercy, O LORD, be upon us, according as we hope in thee.   *Psalm 33:21-22*

Our fathers trusted in thee: they trusted, and thou didst deliver them. They cried unto thee, and were delivered: they trusted in thee, and were not confounded.   *Psalm 22:4-5*

Trust in the LORD, and do good; *so* shalt thou dwell in the land, and verily thou shalt be fed. Delight thyself also in the LORD; and he shall give thee the desires of thine heart. Commit thy way unto the LORD; trust also in him; and he shall bring *it* to pass. And he shall bring forth thy righteousness as the light, and thy judgment as the noonday.   *Psalm 37:3-6*

Blessed *is* that man that maketh the LORD his trust, and respecteth not the proud, nor such as turn aside to lies.   *Psalm 40:4*

And they that know thy name will put their trust in thee: for thou, LORD, hast not forsaken them that seek thee.   *Psalm 9:10*

Wait on God

The LORD *is* good unto them that wait for him, to the soul *that* seeketh him. *It is* good that *a man* should both hope and quietly wait for the salvation of the LORD.
                    Lamentations 3:25-26

Wait on the LORD: be of good courage, and he shall strengthen thine heart: wait, I say, on the LORD.   *Psalm 27:14*

For since the beginning of the world *men* have not heard, nor perceived by the ear, neither hath the eye seen, O God, beside thee, *what* he hath prepared for him that waiteth for him.
Isaiah 64:4

But they that wait upon the LORD shall renew *their* strength; they shall mount up with wings as eagles; they shall run, and not be weary; *and* they shall walk, and not faint.
Isaiah 40:31

Those that wait upon the LORD, they shall inherit the earth...Wait on the LORD, and keep his way, and he shall exalt thee to inherit the land: when the wicked are cut off, thou shalt see *it*.
Psalm 37:9, 34

And therefore will the LORD wait, that he may be gracious unto you, and therefore will he be exalted, that he may have mercy upon you: for the LORD *is* a God of judgment: blessed *are* all they that wait for him.
Isaiah 30:18

Work Diligently

Let ʾ ot your hands be weak: for your work shall be rewarded.
2 Chronicles 15:7

Seest thou a man diligent in his business? he shall stand before kings; he shall not stand before mean *men*.   *Proverbs 22:29*

The thoughts of the diligent *tend* only to plenteousness.   *Proverbs 21:5*

In all labor there is profit.   *Proverbs 14:23*

Wealth *gotten* by vanity shall be diminished: but he that gathereth by labor shall increase.
                                          Proverbs 13:11

Servants, be obedient to them that are *your* masters according to the flesh, with fear and trembling, in singleness of your heart, as unto Christ; Not with eyeservice, as menpleasers; but as the servants of Christ, doing the will of God from the heart; With good will doing service, as to the Lord, and not to men: Knowing that whatsoever good thing any man doeth, the same shall he receive of the Lord.
                                          Ephesians 6:5-8

And whatsoever ye do, do *it* heartily, as to the Lord, and not unto men; Knowing that of the Lord ye shall receive the reward of the inheritance: for ye serve the Lord Christ.
                                          Colossians 3:23-24

His lord said unto him, Well done, *thou* good
and faithful servant: thou hast been faithful
over a few things, I will make thee ruler over
many things: enter thou into the joy of thy
lord.   *Matthew 25:21*

A wise servant shall have rule over a son that
causeth shame, and shall have part of the inheritance among the brethren.   *Proverbs 17:2*

Let a man so account of us, as of the ministers
of Christ, and stewards of the mysteries of
God. Moreover it is required in stewards, that
a man be found faithful...Then shall every man
have praise of God.   *1 Corinthians 4:1-2, 5*

As every man hath received the gift, *even so*
minister the same one to another, as good
stewards of the manifold grace of God.
                                       1 Peter 4:10

Who then is a faithful and wise servant, whom
his lord hath made ruler over his household,
to give them meat in due season? Blessed *is*
that servant, whom his lord when he cometh
shall find so doing. Verily I say unto you, That
he shall make him ruler over all his goods.
                                   Matthew 24:45-47

Study to show thyself approved unto God, a
workman that needeth not to be ashamed,
rightly dividing the word of truth.

2 Timothy 2:15

Special Promises for Me

Special Promises for Me

Special Promises for Me

Special Promises for Me